FINISH FINANCIALLY ⟶ FREE

Copyright © 2023 by Kristi Service Nowrouzi

Published by Kudu Publishing

All rights reserved. No portion of this book may be reproduced, stored in a retrieval system, or transmitted in any form or by any means—electronic, mechanical, photocopy, recording, scanning, or other—except for brief quotations in critical reviews or articles, without prior written permission of the author.
For foreign and subsidiary rights, contact the author.

NMLS #754092 Equal Housing Opportunity

Cover design by Sara Young
Cover Photo by Andrew van Tilborgh

ISBN: 978-1-959095-95-8   1 2 3 4 5 6 7 8 9 10

Printed in the United States of America

IDENTIFY YOUR MONEY BELIEFS
MASTER YOUR MONEY
LIVE IN ABUNDANCE

FINISH FINANCIALLY ⟶ FREE

KRISTI SERVICE NOWROUZI

ALSO BY KRISTI SERVICE NOWROUZI
First Home: Where to Start and How to Win

CONTENTS

Preface vii

Acknowledgments xv

Introduction 17

   CHAPTER 1. **MY STORY** 23

   CHAPTER 2. **OUR BELIEFS ARE THE PROBLEM** 29

   CHAPTER 3. **HABITS WE HAVE FORMED** 67

   CHAPTER 4. **COUPLES AND MONEY** 83

   CHAPTER 5. **MONEY PERSONALITIES** 95

   CHAPTER 6. **PSYCHOLOGY IN MONEY** 109

   CHAPTER 7. **THE BROKE TRAP** 119

   CHAPTER 8. **FINANCIAL LITERACY—THE BASICS** 127

   CHAPTER 9. **RUN YOUR NUMBERS LIKE YOU'RE A BUSINESS** ... 135

   CHAPTER 10. **CREDIT** 159

   CHAPTER 11. **DEBT REPAYMENT** 175

   CHAPTER 12. **CONSIDER YOUR FUTURE** 195

   CHAPTER 13. **ACTION PLAN** 221

   BONUS **RECESSION-PROOF YOUR LIFE** 253

Closing 259

PREFACE

Ohhhhh... seventh grade. Can you remember what it was like to be in middle school? I'm of the age that when I attended it was called junior high school. Seventh grade was the worst year of my life. Not because something tragic happened, but because of the confusing feelings and uncertainty I felt about myself and my place in this world. I was no longer a little kid, and barely a teenager. The boys were maturing at a much slower pace than the girls. And emotionally, we were all a disaster. I had fuzzy, unmanageable hair (and we did a wave thing with our bangs, it was weird), huge braces, acne, a bushy unibrow, and walked pigeon-toed with wobbly knees. Picture that hot mess (notice I didn't put that picture in the book—just describing it is pure torture!).

That was right around the time that I found myself doing nearly anything to try to fit in; although none of us really knew where we fit in or where we belonged. We were raised in not such a great neighborhood, where the influences were not positive. A lot of the kids in my neighborhood were smoking cigarettes and I found myself following the crowd. I was dabbling around fifth or sixth grade, but by seventh grade, this attempt to fit in and be cool had started to take hold and become a habit. Although I didn't see it as a habit, it was part of my daily life. I left home for the bus stop ten minutes early so that we could stop off in the woods and smoke a cigarette or two, usually stolen from a neighbor's parents. I wore a lot of obnoxiously sweet body sprays so my parents couldn't smell it on me.

What started off as an attempt to connect with those around me and help me feel accepted and cool spiraled into a habit and problem that lasted seventeen years. It shaped a big part of my life: I didn't participate in sports, and certain guys wouldn't want to date me because I smoked. I was frequently out on the patio at a bar or party so I could smoke while drinking. It was part of my lifestyle. I quit smoking right after my 30th birthday. It was one of the hardest things I ever did and one of my biggest and proudest accomplishments.

But it was not easy or immediate. I found myself trying dozens of different techniques, one failing attempt after another, until I finally found the one thing that did work. And just for the record, it's not like this "new habit" had taken hold and I was remedied of the old habit twenty-one days later. I remember distinctly, about six months after I quit smoking, reversing out of my driveway and stretching out my arm to pull out a pack of cigarettes from my purse that was laying in the passenger seat. Even six long months later, it was still a force of habit to reach for something that I hadn't touched in 180 days.

Fast forward to a few months ago. I was tagged by a friend in a picture on Facebook. When I went to go and view it, I

PREFACE

thought, "Who is that chubby girl that looks a lot like me?!? Oh shit. That's *me*!"

It wasn't a *bad* picture or terrible angle; it was the reality of the current me. The extra thirty pounds certainly didn't find their way to my body overnight, and neither would they find their way off overnight. But I knew I had to get into action, because the only direction I was headed was toward a larger number on that scale and a bigger dress size. Did I want to dig myself deeper or did I want to start making the right choices to have a positive impact on my life moving forward? My future depended on the answer to that question. Every decision you make today influences your future.

Just like my future depended on it when I knew I had to quit smoking.

Just like my future depended on it about ten years ago when I found myself buried under debt and broke as a joke. I could have either continued getting buried into more debt, just creating a deeper grave, or I could have made the necessary changes to get out from underneath it and live a life that felt freer. Those were my choices. And those are likely your two choices as well.

For my current unwanted circumstances of thirty pounds to shed, I sought out different diet plans and different workout options. I had to go through many before I could find what I felt could work for me. It was the same with smoking, it didn't happen right away, and it didn't work after the first twenty attempts. And to get out of debt, I attempted sooooo many different strategies and suggestions and kept experiencing disappointment after disappointment, getting deeper into debt. It wasn't until I learned some hard lessons, those that I will share with you in this book; that I could finally get past feeling disappointed and experience true change in my beliefs and actions. I imagine you are also seeking what could work for you. There's no magic diet pill and there's no magic get-out-of-debt-free card, either.

What all three of those experiences—smoking, drowning in debt, and being overweight—had in common was that it created suffering in my life, and once I was desperate enough to get rid of it, I created a plan and took action.

You will have to find what works for you. On my quest to change my physical lifestyle, I knew a "diet" would only be a temporary fix, just like being told to pay off your credit cards, It's only a temporary fix. You need a mindset, a way of having an actual relationship with your money, and unless you address it and refine it, you will just find yourself back in the same position again. Being overweight or in debt are symptoms of a problem. We have to address the problem, not focus on the symptoms.

I tried different gyms and different meal plans and different classes. It didn't seem to make much of a difference in my physical state. I ended up visiting a boot camp gym upon a friend's recommendation. I would've never walked in there under any other circumstances. But what I discovered worked for me. I needed the encouragement and coaching of a trainer. I needed the camaraderie and community of the class. I needed the variance that came with custom-created classes that change daily. Going into a gym to complete a circuit of machines wasn't going to cut it.

Let's see if what these pages hold will be just what you are seeking on your road to financial freedom. It's been my personal and professional mission to learn as much as possible about money, finance, credit, and their effect on our lives. I

PREFACE

have studied research from places like the National Endowment for Financial Education (NEFE), who partners with universities to do deep, empirical research on these topics. I have analyzed thousands of credit reports at this point in my career as a mortgage loan officer and a certified credit specialist. I have read literally over a hundred books on money mindset and what shapes our behaviors. I have been to seminars, trainings, workshops, classes, masterminds, and coaching sessions. In the back of this book, I list those that I feel were most impactful, in case you're curious.

Additionally, I have several designations in financial education and specializing in credit knowledge. Finance has been my career for many years, although I am not a financial advisor (by design!), and we will not be talking about products. This experience together will include releasing you from old, deceitful beliefs, allowing you to create a healthy and abundant relationship with money.

We will discover our money personality that will shed light on why you handle money the way you do. We will pinpoint some life habits (financial habits, too) that have taken the driver seat to your daily actions. Also, we will learn how psychology plays a role in our money behaviors and create a vision for your kick-butt life. You are going to dream big and write those dreams down so they become goals, because a dream without a plan is just a wish, so we will formulate a plan that is customized to what you want to accomplish from your working years.

> **You will create a plan, get out of debt, set up a savings plan, and start seeing your dreams get funded!**

FINISH FINANCIALLY FREE

I have a plan to retire at a young enough age to enjoy the "golden years" without worry of how I will pay the bills. I will have the freedom to make choices that include the things that excite me, both now and then. I want to experience really cool places around the world. I want to financially support organizations that I care for. I want to bless my family and friends with thoughtful experiences. All of that takes money and I am living a created plan to allow for all of these things to happen, with ease. What do you desire? I want you to start thinking about your dreams and desires. In a way that you haven't before. Most of us either stopped dreaming or didn't allow ourselves to start dreaming because of how impossible it feels in this current moment.

We are going to get released from those thoughts and lies that hold us back from dreaming and get into action to create the life-altering transformation that will allow you to not only create but live out your dream. It may sound unreal right now, but soon you will start to see all that is possible. But I want to warn you—you can have reasons, or you can have *results*, but you can't have both. I can't remember who said that (first) but it is powerful and true. If you were to list out all the reasons and excuses why you aren't living your most extraordinary life, you will see that none of those are permanent, and many are just self-imposed limitations you believe to be true, but likely aren't. You are going to have to ditch the excuses. If you live in Victimhood, you are hereby evicted.

I wish we could all be a little more honest and vulnerable about how financially broke we are, feeling a little broken, we have made mistakes that make us unsure and less confident in making decisions, and we are likely strangled by debt. For years I was living in a state of crisis, but I didn't let anyone know. Life

PREFACE

is emotional but I have learned we are responsible and have power over our emotions.

As I write this book, I think of my nieces, who range between just out of high school to late twenties. I am writing this book as if I am speaking to one of my precious family members who I love and adore. I am writing this book with the intention to help those in their launching years, from eighteen to thirty-four years old, to your best chance at crushing your goals. However, money beliefs don't discriminate by age. You may be mid-forties or fifties ready to finally take charge of your mind and your money. It's not too late to change your money beliefs so you can live a freer, easier life going forward. Cheers to this first step of finishing financially free. I am so glad you are here with me.

ACKNOWLEDGMENTS

I give all the glory to God! First and foremost, I thank our loving God, who calls us His children. He loves me, and He loves you, too, and wants you to know it.

This book is dedicated to the amazing people in my life. Because of you, I have the confidence to put my thoughts and knowledge on paper and share it with the world, in spite of slurs and insults because of differing viewpoints.

Thank you to my husband, for your constant support and encouragement. I love you.

Thank you momma, for being my #1 cheerleader, always. God gave me the best gift when he created me in your womb. You are truly the most special woman on the planet.

Thank you to my family. My sisters, brothers, and their awesome spouses, parents-in-law, aunts, my incredible chosen daughter Tamara, and nieces and nephews. I am so proud of you and so grateful for you. Your love is real and our bond is deep, and I will never take for granted how safe and special that is. You are such a blessing and I love you.

Thank you to my incredible friends. You make life so amazing and fulfilling because of our love and friendship. How boring it might be without you outrageous people in my life! Thank you Jaime, Jenna, Missty, Ci-Gee and Joe, Jeff and Katy, Tiffany, Jen, Tim, Madison, Jessi, Mary, Kimmie, Tom, Megan, Dana—may we play and have fun until we are 101!

Thank you to my partners—because of your trust and partnership, together we served our clients with high standards of care and professionalism. A special thank you Chris, Kat, John, Tom, Nallita, Adam, Ronda, Anderson, Jake, Ben, Norma, and Nick for the many years of synergy.

Thank you to my mentors, many know they are strong examples of leadership and inspiration, and many have no idea of how impactful they are, even though I tell you and thank you!

Thank you for thought leaders like Tony Robbins who have ignited something in me to find and develop my passions. To grow in thought and knowledge every day. To be open to new ideas, even when I feel like I should hold on tightly to what I think I believe, you have taught me to be open to and hungry for new possibilities.

Thank you, dear reader. Thank you for investing your valuable time in what I have to share. My prayer for you is that this book is a very positive impact in your life.

INTRODUCTION

Money is a funny thing. It can pay for the most extraordinary experiences and also cause a lot of struggles in relationships. It can keep us in jobs we hate or keep us up at night stressing about how we are going to make ends meet. The amount of money one makes can also dictate our friends. Think about it, do you see a lot of broke people hanging out with rich friends? They wouldn't be able to keep up; not only with the material things like "keeping up with the Joneses" but they also wouldn't be able to afford the travel, dinners, and events that people with money might regularly enjoy.

Money is something we cannot escape or ignore in our lives; we exchange about a third of our time in our adult life for money. There is almost nothing in life that money doesn't touch, yet most people get *really uncomfortable* talking about money. Money and sex rank as the top two most intimate and personal topics, and both can have very significant impacts on our lives. There's a good chance your parents didn't teach you about money, nor did you really learn how to master money from school. I think most people are not taught about money because most people don't know enough to teach it. Schools teach us how to be obedient, learn enough to be contributing humans in society, and follow rules so we can be decent employees. If you do a quick search online on the origin of our education system, you can see for yourself that it was mostly created to make us into . . . good workers.

Even in the Bible, work and money are mentioned hundreds of times, so these have been important topics since the dawn of time. Even Adam "worked" in the Garden of Eden. I share this with you because we are created to work, and our work should provide us with reward. But for many people, it's exhausting rather than rewarding. In our daily lives, we exchange our time, value, and expertise for money—our financial reward. It's rarely a "fair trade" since we can't get that time back; it's not a renewable source (like money is). And for most of the population, what we bring home and what we spend are misaligned with each other.

> **The sad truth is that it's not only about how much we make. It's about what we do with what we earn.**

Do you ever feel like there is more month than money? That no matter what amount you save it goes to something else (surprise bills or an emergency), so there always seems to be nothing left? No matter what you cut out of your budget it just doesn't seem to be enough. When there isn't enough money, life can feel out of control. All over headlines, it seems that many

INTRODUCTION

people are living paycheck to paycheck, haven't started saving for retirement, are behind where they should be for their age in savings and contributing towards retirement vessels, have less than $1,000 in the bank. . . . the depressing list goes on and on. Add to that the crazy costs of housing, how much it costs monthly for car payments on a decent car, credit card debt, and outstanding student loans. No wonder we don't talk about money—what's good about it?!

The sad truth is that it's not only about how much we make. It's about what we do with what we make. How we spend and what we save. Easy to say, difficult to live out. I totally get it. I lived the same struggle for too many years. I used to say, "If I only earned $10,000 more a year, then I could . . ." Does this sound familiar? Fill in the blank: "If only I could . . . get out of debt, start my retirement account, save, have a buffer so I don't have pennies in the bank account before payday, etc. If only . . .

It's not the $10,000. I got a $10,000 raise and guess what happened? I bet you guessed it. I spent it. As my income increased, so did my spending. I was simply financing my lifestyle. Society has made this the norm. Think about it. We finance our homes, cars, furniture, cell phones, tires, and even our pets. If you get that raise, there's a really good chance you will spend it by adding another purchased desire and therefore increasing your monthly bills, like buying a new toy (financed, of course) or buying a higher-priced car or home.

I have seen doctors and attorneys and those who make incomes in the top 5 percent of income earners, who finance everything! They lease expensive cars, live in expensive homes, and have expensive toys but what many don't have are savings. What you see on the outside (the stuff) is not typically reflective of what you may see on the inside (savings). It's a social norm to spend high dollars for what we yearn to have—status and acceptance.

> **It's not about money; it's about status and acceptance.**

I share this with you because what I see makes my heart hurt. As a mortgage loan officer, I get to analyze your entire financial picture. And I have seen thousands and thousands at this point in my career. I get to see aspects that even financial advisors don't typically see because they don't look at credit reports when meeting with and advising their clients But I do. I see borrowing habits, incomes, and spending habits. I see your bank statements and where your money goes. Financial advisors don't look at these things. They usually don't even see your paystubs. I have an insider's viewpoint and I see what has become commonplace.

A long time ago, I remember reading (paraphrased), "Show me someone's bank statement (transactions) and their calendar, and I can tell you what they are committed to." Those two things show where you put your time, money, and energy. There is a real problem—*debt*—that has become normal for many people, but it is suffocating us. We have to make changes. The economy may force that change for many. So, let's get ahead of it so it doesn't hurt.

If you're looking for a book that will teach you which stocks to pick or how much to diversify in your portfolio, this isn't the book for you. But if you are looking to understand why you have certain beliefs about money, how your behaviors affect you today and shape your tomorrow, and how to finally take

INTRODUCTION

charge of your financial situation so you can stop losing sleep and stressing to the point of physical illness, let's take this journey together. No more living paycheck to paycheck. No more putting off dreams or worse—not even allowing yourself to dream because you feel trapped with no money.

This is About Healthy Financial Thinking

This book will be your guide to uncovering your deeply ingrained beliefs you have about money. Then, you can understand your money personality. Then you will be able to create a new relationship with money, where you are the one directing how it works for you, not money directing you to work for it. You have to know yourself to grow yourself.

The first part of this book will be focused on discovering your beliefs about money, identifying your behavior and habits with money, and understanding what money *really* is. I am going to assume that since we all have such different experiences in our past, it would be difficult to create money examples that everyone can relate to. Many people reading this book may not have lived on their own yet; they may still be living with their parents or with a partner/spouse and getting ready to take on that endeavor on their own for the first time. Many others may have made mistake after financial mistake because no one has taught them about money, nor has there been a good example to mimic. There are so many different money behaviors (over-spenders, over-savers, scaredy-cats, or risky choices) that it could become exhaustive to list enough examples that you could connect with. Therefore, I am going to use examples of what many of us can relate to—experiences such as weight loss diets or quitting/creating a habit.

The second part of this book will take on more of a teaching tone to help create your action plan based on your big dreams and goals. You've got those, don't you? They may feel buried down deep inside of you. We are going to bring them to your focus and create a plan for you to accomplish all that you want to and create the kind of life you desire. It's going to take more than just paying off your credit cards. It's going to require more than just the income you earn from your job. This part of the book will help you to create ideas and action steps to not only eliminate debt but the behaviors that create debt. It will also help you learn how to make your money make money and create passive income. Wealth won't happen to most of us through winning the lottery or getting some big inheritance. So, let's create wealth through steps and strategies that we control. That we put into place. That we can get excited about because of the results we can actually obtain.

Before we dive into all that I want to teach you, I think it's important for you to know who I am, why I wrote this book, and why I am so extremely passionate about sharing ideas and knowledge about how we relate to money and finances.

CHAPTER 1

MY STORY

Although I don't like talking about myself, especially the parts of my past I'm not especially proud of, I feel like it's important that you know who I am. We all have a journey, a story, and I believe God uses all of it to help build our character, grow us to fulfill our purpose, and use it to encourage others through their own journey. And when it comes to money, each of us learned our money lessons in such different ways. What we have learned has become our money story. It creates the behaviors and habits that we exercise every day. My money story definitely showed up every day, and it kept me stuck. Before I share with you how I uncovered my money story (and how you will uncover yours), I want to share a little of my young adult years with you.

The day I turned fifteen, I went and got my driver's permit and applied for my first job. My family was poor most of my childhood and I had friends that had . . . things. They wore the best clothes, had a car waiting for them when they turned sixteen, wore shoes I envied and wanted, and enjoyed great family vacations. I wanted those things, too, but there was only one way that was going to happen, and that depended on me.

My parents did gift me my first car. It was the most they ever were able to spend on me, and I got a stick shift, hatchback, no-radio-or-AC-car while living in Florida. But it ran, and that was all that mattered! I could get myself to school and work instead of my mom waiting outside the mall every evening and weekend to get me home from work. But that cheap car wasn't what I wanted, because it didn't equal the cars my friends were getting. While I should have been extremely grateful for this first ride, I was saving toward something . . . better. I had four cars in high school because I was striving to get to where my friends were at. Sad, I know. But even more pathetic is that I spent the next fifteen years playing the same game, trying to get better, faster, more expensive, prettier, the next brand up . . . you get the point. And for what? External things do not get you "accepted" by others. If that is what it takes, then perhaps re-evaluate who you call friends. I was obsessed with looking like I had money. Because I'd never had money before. So, I played the part, externally, while spending all of my time working. The more I spent, the more I wanted and the more I had to work to pay for it. I worked multiple jobs, even in high school.

I put myself through college at the pace of a snail. Because I was so obsessed in high school with earning money, my grades were barely average. Nothing exceptional and nothing worthy of scholarships (or even being accepted into a university, so I didn't even try). I started off at community college while

MY STORY

working full-time. I eventually finished the last two years of my bachelor's degree at a college that offered evening and weekend classes, as this school catered to working adults. I definitely didn't get to experience the college dorm and party life.

I was also taking on student loan debt and driving a car that was way too expensive for the little money I earned working various jobs at minimum wage. Barely getting by financially was a way of life for me. And it never dawned on me that the cool car that sat in the parking lot at my job didn't define me or my identity. Yet, I still paid way too much each month for it (compared to what I was earning).

Once I finished college and started earning some decent money, I also found myself spending more. Every time I earned more, I spent more. I got a fancier car, a fancier home, and fancier wardrobe. All financed with too large of a mortgage, a high car payment, and many credit cards that had a high balance that I simply fed with minimum payments to stay in good standing. If I did put a large payment on a credit card balance, I rewarded my great efforts with a shopping spree (increasing that balance again). It never dawned on me to save or even have a plan for my money. What certainly didn't help was I started to do drugs to fuel my energy and party atmosphere. I got caught up in an unhealthy relationship that revolved around cocaine and way too much alcohol. Then, the global financial crisis hit, and I was probably the most unprepared for it. I was spending money like it was never going to cease coming in, financing everything, and not saving; it punched me in the face.

I lost almost everything—my relationship (which actually was a good thing), my career, my home that I had to short sale to avoid foreclosure, and any confidence I had. I finally was "making money" but I didn't have a plan, I didn't have guidance, and I obviously didn't know what I was doing—although on the outside, prior to that moment, you would have thought I had my life together. What a fraud and fake. I had people fooled, but I knew deep down inside that I was just faking it. It's a terrible thing to endure, to lose everything and have to start all over. I have watched a lot of people over the years lose everything and start all over, but not learn lessons from their mistakes. I chose to learn from my prior experience and choices and do things differently. My hope is that you will learn from my mistakes so you don't have to learn the lessons the hard way or learn to learn from your mistakes so you can change your actions and not stay suck in a rut, destined to repeat the lesson.

I will be sharing with you a lot of lessons learned. Some lessons are from those experiences but also a lot from my clients. I have met so many people who are drowning in debt. Choked by monthly payments that are mostly eaten up by interest, the balances don't go down by much. They have no savings, no emergency fund, maxed-out credit cards, and a poor credit profile. It's actually not uncommon, and this is *not* good that it is the "normal" for so many people. Life is not blissful when we are a slave to debt and have to work in jobs we don't love because "we need the paycheck." I have been broke as a joke (literally—living off bean burritos and buying my shampoo and body wash at the dollar store because I had to) and plush with cash. I can promise you those are two very different feelings and I want you to experience ease in your finances, too!

I am not a financial advisor, and I am not going to be talking about what stocks to choose or what mutual fund may have the most impressive returns. This is the good news—because financial advisors sell products with the goal of investing and growing your money, and I am not here to sell you a product.

MY STORY

When you have money stored up and ready to invest, consider going to a financial advisor—someone who you know and trust recommends. I have a financial advisor and most wealthy people have a trusted financial advisor. But that is not our focus right now. Right now, we are going to gain understanding, have some ah-ha moments, and then create a simple plan to follow.

I started off barely surviving in college, scraping by but not thoroughly enjoying my twenties figuring some things out but getting by my own way in my thirties. And now, in my forties, and really paying attention to my own actions (and lessons learned), I am going to teach you and share with you all of the lessons I learned throughout my journey and also in my line of work to help you start thriving and enjoying money. Let's stop getting our butts kicked. Finally.

CHAPTER 2

OUR BELIEFS ARE THE PROBLEM

The problem is evident. Isn't it? We need more money. "If I could just win the lottery." "If I could just make $10k more per year." "If I could just get that promotion, if I had any of those things all of my problems would go away." The problem may not be how much you earn—although more might definitely help! Instead, the problem might have more to do with your beliefs about money. If you believe you aren't worthy of money, you can't handle money, or you are no good with money or numbers, then that is what will prove to be true. Whatever we believe is likely what we will keep living. If we believe money is in short supply, that's likely how it will play out in our lives. If we believe we aren't smart about money, it will be hard to break out of that and learn about handling money in a way that gets us ahead. Having the wrong beliefs about money keeps us stuck and broke. These are examples of the "problem" of our beliefs. Knowing what you believe about money isn't enough. We will need to answer the question about why those beliefs are a problem which we will explore and uncover in this chapter.

There is power in language. When you say, "I can't," your mind believes you because you are the boss of your mind. When someone else says, "You can't," you may receive that as a challenge and feel like you have something to prove. But when *you* say and own "I can't," then... your mind allows you to prove yourself right. It's always seeking ways to prove you right. Words have power.

> **Whether you think you can or think you can't, you are right. —Henry Ford**

I ask you not to just blindly believe every word I type, but to consider some thoughts and ideas that you may not have considered before. I am going to share some thoughts and ideas that might resonate with you, and I may share some things that may contradict your beliefs. And that is okay. I give you permission not to accept everything I say as truth.

I will be sharing teachings and concepts I have learned along the way from masterful mentors, extraordinary leaders, and influential gurus. But I don't *always* agree with *everything* they teach. Take out of this what is meant for you. But also acknowledge that sometimes when something is disturbing to hear, it might be *exactly* what you need to learn to have amazing breakthroughs in your life.

I am not going to accept an average life, feel stuck, or waste my life away because of fears or self-limiting beliefs, and I hope you feel the same way. Also consider just knowing something isn't enough. We all know how to lose weight—work out and have a healthy diet. Yet most Americans are overweight. We all know how to save money—spend less than you make and put extra aside. It's the implementation of the knowledge that matters. When it's time to get into action, I will make it simple to implement so that you can actually begin to make a positive impact on your life, and who knows, maybe even the lives of future generations.

The Problem is We Believe We Shouldn't Have Problems

Let's get back to our beliefs. Most of what we believe is either what our environment and upbringing told us to believe or the result of lessons learned. We have either chosen to accept something or unconsciously accepted a belief to be true. Many of our beliefs come from what our parents or caretakers taught us, but unfortunately some of what we believe is based on lies and hurtful words from others. Did you hear words or go through an experience that led you to believe something that you know isn't truth, although you treated it as truth? Most of us do. A few examples might be, "No one will ever love you because you are unlovable." "You'll never succeed at . . ." "Why even try, it's not even possible." Some of those are words that sadly we may have been told, and some of those may have been self-created based on a failure or hurt. It repeats and repeats to protect yourself from being put in that position of feeling that pain again. But these are lies that might keep us from even trying (to take a risk) again. These beliefs shape what we think and the actions we take, but beliefs aren't the only thing that controls our thoughts and actions. Our personalities have a big impact, too.

Our most formative years are between ages four and six, and during those formative years, the main elements of our core personality begin to take shape. However, our personality is still being developed beyond childhood. According to research, our individual personality is shaped by our genetics and our environment, such as where we live, cultural and spiritual influences, family, friends, and experiences. Finances, education, and even body type can have an impact on the shaping of your personality. Who we are at our core, as in our personality, is mostly set by age twenty-one. That's not to say that life experiences, trauma, and growth doesn't happen after twenty-one, but most of our underlying ways of being and beliefs are deeply rooted by the time we reach our early twenties.

Most personality traits don't easily change, although they can be altered. For example, if arrogance or aggression is a strong personality type in a person, it doesn't mean they cannot learn new ways of relating to personality traits they would like to demonstrate, such as patience and kindness. For more information on personality traits, you can research personality traits to uncover your strongest traits. But personality traits are more difficult to change than beliefs.

When you were a young child, did you believe in Santa Claus? Was it easy to believe Santa wasn't real once someone exposed to you that Santa was a tale? Remember, beliefs are something we have either accepted to be true or had an experience that led us to believe a certain thing. If I haven't been able to save money before, I might believe I am unable to save money. But there is a way to create a new belief and then live into that belief. If you could create a way to save just $10 every month, you could create a new belief that you can save money each month and build on that belief through actions that result in support of the new belief (a savings account that is growing each month).

Our behaviors and attitudes show up in our actions. And our actions are what create habits. We are going to dive deep into habits in an upcoming chapter, but I want to show you how all of this ties together. So, if you have tried to make some positive change in the past and didn't experience success, perhaps it was because you weren't addressing the proper aspect. Now you see how one can impact the others.

Our personality is what we are.
Our beliefs are what we think.
Our behaviors are how we express ourselves.
Our attitudes are how we approach things—our state of mind or way of being.
Our actions are what we do.

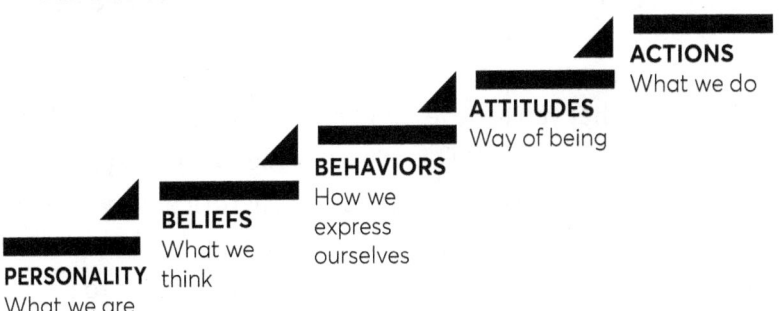

All of these things listed above have become second nature. When how we show up each day is just automatic and pre-programmed, always just being a certain way, we can see how we just get into a routine and often stay there. I am not out to change your personality, because that is what uniquely makes up *wonderful* you. It's the focus of this book to address our beliefs, which flows into our behaviors, which alters our attitudes, which impacts our actions. Replacing money beliefs that don't serve you well with those that will grow you will ultimately change your life's trajectory and have you walking right into living out your dreams.

Changing your belief, something that is so deeply ingrained, can be difficult because our beliefs are just automatic. By uncovering what you believe to be true about money that may not be serving you well may create new perspective, and perhaps you will feel confident replacing a belief with one that better serves you. Think of this as an upgrade.

Everything in My Life is Shaped by My Beliefs (Which Were Shaped by Others)

What is it that you believe about money? What do you believe to be true about money? This is very personal and highly emotional. I don't want you to ask this in a rhetorical way. I really want you to pause, right now, and just ponder... *what is it that I believe about money?* This next statement is going to sound harsh, but I think it's true: Most people don't stop to think about what they are thinking about. We just go through the motions, allowing past voices that said what they said to become that inside voice we listen to as if it is truth. We are (intentionally or not) too distracted to stop and think about what we are thinking about. Let's get into a habit of taking our thoughts captive. If a thought doesn't empower you or serve you well—if it's not

OUR BELIEFS ARE THE PROBLEM

encouraging or empowering—then counter that thought with its opposite. If the thought is "I always mess things up" then replace that thought with "I have a new opportunity to make this happen the way I desire." Put the brakes on autopilot and take this moment to think about what your beliefs about money have always been.

Think of what you often say or think when it comes to money. In order to really see this more clearly, maybe take a step back and go further back in your timeline. What was your environment like growing up when it came to money? Most of us, if we really thought deeply enough about it, can have memories around money conversations and experiences as young as four years old. What did your parents or caretakers demonstrate to you about money?

I always experienced not having enough (sometimes it was said, sometimes it was expressed, and sometimes through actual lived experience). *"Money doesn't grow on trees. We can't afford that. How do you think we would pay for that? I need Friday (payday) to be here. Rich people are selfish."*

So, what was your experience? What money conversations did you commonly hear? Or were there just no conversations about money at all? Was money considered evil? Did it cause fights? Did it cause stress in your family? Or did it seem easy for your parents or caretakers to pay bills and afford their desires?

My experience was that we just didn't have a lot. And might not *ever* have a lot. We lived below the poverty level for the first many years of my life. But my parents always had food on the table and kept the electricity on (except that one time!). I wore hand-me-downs and ate lots of casseroles, because they filled us up and could feed a large family for cheap. We all have a past, but it doesn't have to be our future. . . . except that it can/might/will be if we don't question our beliefs; otherwise, we will keep living in the past.

I want to challenge you again to stop for a bit here. Think about what it is you believe about money, because there is a really good chance that you are living that belief and don't even know it! And I want to take a moment and acknowledge that this is hard work to dig deep like this. I know when I "reflect" on the past, I often just relive the pain that past decisions and circumstances have caused. Who wants to relive that crap? But try and recall what you learned through your environment and the actions of others you learned from. We can learn a ton from patterns. I see a lot of generational patterns. If you stop to think about your grandparents, what similarities do you see in your parents that may have been the patterns of their parents? Look around in your life and perhaps at your parents or those who raised you and your siblings, if you have any. Can you spot generational patterns? Can you learn from watching those patterns? What patterns are showing up in your life that you can correlate back to beliefs you acquired as a child?

On the next page, I have included a worksheet I created for a video-led course that really dives deep into this question. We need to peel back these protective layers because they are likely keeping you stuck. They are there with the intention of keeping you safe and secure and keeping you from change and the scary unknown. But those layers are keeping you from growing past a tantrum-throwing four-year-old that may be holding your financial greatness hostage. Let's spend some time exploring what is possible.

OUR BELIEFS ARE THE PROBLEM

UNCOVERING YOUR CORE STORY

Note that the first answers that your mind provides to these questions are going to be superficial. It's a protective mechanism. It's a way to keep you safe; remain in survival mode. Once you start uncovering these layers, go back and re-read each question, and see if there is a deeper, more powerful answer you can now give. Sometimes it takes going back through this exercise four, five, or six times to uncover a deeper answer. But that is where the truth is found. Remember, these decisions you made about money were made when you were likely 4-6 years old.

You have been living an unquestioned belief for all of these years since. It may take 2 hours and many times going back to the beginning, but remember you are uncovering years of living into a belief. Be real to yourself. Only you can take ownership—you can't change or fix what you don't own.

Let's have the courage, together, to face it. Ready to let it go? Let's do this:

What did your mother think about money? _____
_____

What did your father think about money? _____
_____

How did they interact (or act) about money (or lack thereof)?
_____

What is your most painful memory associated with money?
_____
_____

FINISH FINANCIALLY FREE

If you don't have a painful memory, what earliest memory do you have about money, perhaps you saw a parent(s) or a relative do something about money (hide money, fight about money, etc.)?
_____

What (do you think you) were you taught was most important about money? _____
_____

When you think about money, what do you worry about?
_____

What is your BIGGEST fear about money? Our fears fuel your core story. _____
_____

What's the worst-case scenario related to money? _____
_____

Where do you feel a loss of power/control? _____
_____

What do you secretly wish were true about money? _____
_____

What do you secretly fear may be true in revealing your story?
_____

We all have different behaviors when it comes to money. It's based on the Money Personality (and it is likely a mix, not just one Money Personality) you default to. In chapter 5 you will find the definitions of Money Personalities and look to identify with your own dominant personality type. I have put into one category several closely related personalities to keep things streamlined. Something in your life may have changed your behaviors as you go through life (divorce, a death of a loved one, job loss) and has you feeling insecure or unstable where perhaps you didn't give money much thought before.

When I first worked through these questions, I learned something that I never knew existed. You see, my parents (who are awesome, by the way) gave and provided for so many. My father was a pastor and principal/teacher at a small Christian church/school in Idaho, and my mother raised five kids, ran a daycare from our home, and took in hundreds of foster kids (yes, *hundreds*—you read that right!). They helped take care of friends and neighbors in need and even housed traveling missionaries. They did so much good, and yet, we were poor. From that experience, I took on a core belief that I could do good in this world (as demonstrated by them) OR make money. I didn't believe I could have both. The examples in my environment didn't show me or teach me that. I thought it was an OR and not an AND. Not knowing this belief is what kept me broke. Learning of, acknowledging, and releasing this belief changed my whole life. This is called your money story or money script.

Who Was Supposed to Teach Us About Money?

FINISH FINANCIALLY FREE

What is your money story? I have seen families that seemed to "have it all" only to learn later it was all just financed and they were one missed paycheck from broke. I have friends who are so scared of being broke that they squander every penny earned above their modest lifestyle, at the cost of fun and experiences and occasional treats, just to never have to feel broke again (but almost living as if they are poor).

I remember a friend in high school always getting money from her mom and being told, "Don't tell your dad." Why was this a secret and what was that teaching my friend about money and communication? I think it left her confused, like, "Why would dad have a problem with you slipping me twenty dollars for the weekend? What does dad have against a little play money?" I believe that most couples don't fight about *money*; they just don't understand their own beliefs about money. We can't talk about what we don't understand. We just keep behaving the way we always have because it got us this far. That can create a lot of tension in a relationship. But how do you talk about something you have perhaps never questioned nor learned about?

> **If you can't envision what your life will look like, then you can't design it in your thinking and in this foundational work.**

My hope is that you have uncovered a few unknown beliefs you had about money. You may have found that you have several money stories. If you have found that you have several stories, make sure you work through the dominant story worksheet (page 37-38) as this is likely the belief that leads your unconscious thinking. Now that you have brought this story into your awareness, we can create empowering language around those beliefs that may now better serve you.

Keep in mind as we go through this book that your past and present environments shape your identity and beliefs, as do the words that those around you have said that you believe as truth. I know of people whose grandparents shared *their* beliefs about money, and then their *parents* adopted those beliefs, and then they *themselves* adopted those same beliefs. What grandma or grandpa experienced and believed does not have to be your story. Look for those patterns.

Make sure the voice you listen to is one that is encouraging truth, not based on the past or even old fables. Yeah, I said it. Grandparents were influenced by their experiences and their caretakers, their upbringing, environment and neighborhood, and culture. It was a very different era. My father was born during the Great Depression in the 1930s and his experiences don't have to be mine. Some things may have been taught to you with the intention of keeping you protected but instead kept you stuck. Let's let those old stories and experiences go and write a fresh story.

Are You Willing to Give Up Who You Are Today to Become Who You Want to Be?

It's also important to say that as you are working through old beliefs, it may become quite emotional for you. Beliefs are tied to emotions. So, if something gets triggered and you feel some old feelings from the past, give yourself permission to free yourself of those beliefs. Let them go, but you have to replace those old beliefs with new beliefs.

This starts with believing that you are worthy of having money. You are capable of having your money work for you. If you put it to work, you deserve the reward (so many people believe they deserve "it," whatever "it" is to them, because so much marketing communicates this—you deserve "it" just because and without working for "it"). So put in the work that will reward you handsomely.

If you can't envision what your life will look like, then you can't design it in your thinking and in this foundational work. Start seeing yourself enjoying experiences and life's finer treasures with those you love. Believe it is for you. And it is possible. Start seeing the future you intend to live.

Now that you have uncovered some important past beliefs, let's ask a new question. What do you value about money and what do you want it to do for you? _____

_____

_____

Spend just a few minutes here. Think about it. Ask it out loud. Write it out. However you do it, don't skip this. On a superficial level, what might come up first are the easy answers. But those aren't the driver of your values. Sure, you don't want to stress anymore, you want to buy whatever you want, whenever you want to. But go deeper. Because chances are, that isn't *actually* what you want. There's a much deeper meaning. Don't believe me? Hear me out. This is just a belief you have created that I want to help dispel.

It's easy to want to just buy things that make us feel good, feel important, or look good to others. It feels good to have something other people might want to have themselves or to look a certain way (like a rich person or a person of status). At first that might sound or look appealing, but it is actually so much deeper than that. It's about: feeling like you are in control, that you can make empowering decisions, and you do not have limitations to your dreams. Money can create opportunities to bless others, to have enjoyable experiences, and feel a more justified trade-off for our time exchange of money. Money doesn't create fulfillment or importance. Look around—there are many rich people who aren't "important" and there are many unfulfilled people who have a lot of money.

It's important to get to the root of what you want, because then you will start to learn a little more about yourself. What I have found working through answering this question is that most people want to create incredible life experiences that will make amazing memories for themselves and those they love (instead of just having money to pay bills) and to feel like they are in control of their money, not the other way around.

What do you value about money and what do you want it to do for you?

Personally, I was always chasing money. But money—the actual paycheck I earned—was spent before I received it. And if I was getting a bonus or overtime, I had it assigned to something before I actually got paid. The more I made, the more I spent. When I asked myself, "What do I value about money?" For me, it was freedom. All I really wanted was to get to the point where I didn't have to look at my checking account balance first to agree to go out to lunch. Seriously, the feeling of seeing just $10 in your bank account sucks. I hated the anxiety of paying my bills and not knowing if I had enough to pay them all when they were due. I hated the stress of late fees and wondering if it was going to be reported late on my credit report.

I want freedom, freedom to actually go someplace on vacation because I have the money to do so. I want to create experiences and enjoy my time outside of work, not sit at home because I spent my entire paycheck and don't have money for fun things. Freedom. More money wasn't the answer. The answer was not blowing all of it the moment I got it. I was a slave instead of a master. Know the feeling? So, what do you want money to do for you?

By spending some time on these questions and really uncovering what you have believed in the past and what you desire to believe for the creation of your desired future, you will release years of lies you have accepted and lived through as truth. This will open up space to create a new and empowering belief system that will serve you well instead of holding you back.

Let go of the old B.S. (Belief System)!

Now that we have uncovered a few layers of the beliefs and the deception those beliefs have created, let's look at how the words we speak and think have power in our lives. Words Have Power!

Before we move to the next topic and chapter, I do want to focus on the words we use and who we listen to. All day long,

OUR BELIEFS ARE THE PROBLEM

we are listening to others: family, friends, colleagues, experts, news outlets, influencers, and the list goes on. The words we hear from others can become an inner voice that guides our thoughts, behaviors, and actions. Make sure what you listen to from other people is empowering, not reducing your self-worth. And pay attention to the way you speak to yourself. If I could hear your inner voice, what would I hear? If you wouldn't say those words to your best friend, don't allow your inner voice to say them to you.

So, let's take a look at the words we use as some of them are not synonyms, although we often use them as such.

BROKE AND POOR

There is a difference between broke and poor. I think everyone should experience being broke, once in their life. It's humbling. It can create compassion and empathy when we see someone else in that situation. But don't stay there for long, as being broke can take hold of your identity and keep you stuck and stressed. Overall, the average American is broke and living outside of their means; meaning they don't have excess money for an emergency, are swimming in debt, and don't have a considerable, growing savings account. That's broke.

Living in poverty (poor) is about not earning enough to pay for life's absolute basic necessities (shelter, food, electricity). For those living in poverty, there doesn't seem to be a way out, and it is long-term (often their entire lifetime) and often multi-generational. There are billions of people around the globe who are poor. The majority of Americans are broke and *choosing* to live outside of their means. Please know there is a difference between poor and broke and we need to respect the distinction. Being poor means not having the means needed to survive and thrive. Being broke is not managing what money you do have.

RICH AND WEALTHY

There is a difference between rich and wealthy, too. Rich means able to pay for needs and wants; everyone has a different definition of what "rich" means to them. Wealthy means owning assets and not *having* to work for money. There are plenty of rich people, meaning they earn a substantial income, but if they spend it all (and plenty of people are spending and borrowing at excessive rates, often outspending their income to finance their lifestyle), they could also be on their way to broke. What happens if their income stops? Would you say that someone earning $250,000 per year is rich? Most of us would say yes because it is nearly in the top 5 percent of wage earners. I read in a recent survey that over 36 percent of those who earned over $250,000 a year said they were living paycheck to paycheck. Well, isn't that kind of the definition of broke? Having nothing left?

The rich often have no or negative net worth because their assets are over-leveraged by debt (liabilities). The U.S. is rich compared to most countries, yet we are less happy than other countries. Being rich does not equate to being happy.

Wealthy people not only have enough money to meet their needs and enjoy their wants, but they have a substantial net worth. What is net worth? The simplest definition I know to share is that net worth is the value of something minus any debt on it. In business, we hear it called assets and liabilities. Assets can be real estate, cash, investments, a business, and just . . . stuff that has a value like cars, art, furniture, etc. Liabilities are the loans, costs, taxes, and such that go against the assets. Wealthy people have high net worth and often don't have to work any longer to earn money. Their money earns money for them and they often have created passive income (cash flow they don't have to work for, more on this later in the book). THIS—this is where you desire to be.

Wealthy People Own Assets, But Broke People Own Debt

But many if not most rich people can't get wealthy because of their appetite to spend and satisfy their wants. The rich tend to spend, and the wealthy tend to save and invest. The wealthy tend to have a long view of investing and also make wiser money choices that allow them to stay wealthy.

I want to share with you the three socio-economic categories that are out of R.K. Payne's book *A Framework for Understanding Poverty: A Cognitive Approach for Educators, Policymakers, Employers and Service Providers*.[1] The author compares more categories than those listed below; however, I wanted to show you the comparison of how each class views (generally speaking) the topic. Really study how each group views very important topics such as money, education, family, and ultimately how they view their ultimate destiny. I would encourage you to read each group vertically the first time you view this, and then horizontally across each topic to really compare and contrast the various viewpoints.

---

[1] R.K. Payne, *A Framework for Understanding Poverty: A Cognitive Approach for Educators, Policymakers, Employers, and Service Providers*, sixth edition (United States, aha! Process, 2018).

FINISH FINANCIALLY FREE

TOPIC	POVERTY	MIDDLE CLASS	WEALTHY
Possessions	People	Things	One-of-a-kind objects, legacies
Money	To be used, spent	To be managed	To be conserved, invested
Education	Valued and revered as abstract but not as reality	Crucial for climbing success ladder and making money	Necessary tradition for making and maintaining connections
Family Structure	Tends to be matriarchal	Tends to be patriarchal	Depends on who has money
Driving Force	Survival, relationships, entertainment	Work, achievement	Financial, political, social connections
Language	Language is about survival	Language is about negotiation	Language is about networking
Destiny	Believes in fate Cannot do much to mitigate chance	Believes in choice Can change future with good choices now	Noblesse oblige With wealth, power, and prestige come responsibility

What stood out to you in this comparison? Our beliefs about money shape our experience of money. And probably more important than that, it shapes our experience of life and our world. For me, the one that hits the hardest is "destiny"—to believe that fate, and not your choices and actions, are in control versus being responsible for my destiny. And when you don't have money, the relationship with money can often feel stressful and painful and your future looks dismal.

An absolutely awesome read is *The Millionaire Next Door: The Surprising Secrets of America's Wealthy* by Thomas J. Stanley and William D. Danko.[2] Although there is a newer book called *The **Next** Millionaire Next Door* by Thomas J. Stanley and Sarah

---

2 Thomas J. Stanley and William D. Danko, *The Millionaire Next Door: The Surprising Secrets of America's Wealthy* (Taylor Trade Publishing, 2010).

OUR BELIEFS ARE THE PROBLEM

Stanley Fallaw,[3] I feel it is lacking some of the fundamental teachings the original book demonstrates (although the first book is a bit dated, *The Millionaire Next Door*[4] still has some great takeaways about how the wealthy actually live, which may surprise you).

Now that you know the difference between rich and wealthy, maybe you have decided that you should decrease your debt or that you should determine where you are overspending in a way that's not being true to your desires. Perhaps these distinctions in the words got you excited about creating true wealth and passive income (later in this book I will share more on this topic) and you have learned that "rich" is not the end goal.

If something is really important to you, truly important as far as a goal to accomplish, remove the word "should" and replace it with "must." When you say you *should*, you are implying a hope for something. You are saying... maybe. It's not definite and it's not probable.

Instead, replace it with the word *must*. If you must earn more money, you *must* get that degree or certificate, hone that skill, update the resume, or simply stop wasting hours each night streaming mindless shows so you can focus on next steps to increasing your income (working a better-paying shift, creating passive income, etc.). Must means all in, will do, consider it in action, get out of my way! Must is definitive.

Stop "Shoulding" on Yourself!

---

[3] Thomas J. Stanley and Sarah Stanley Fallaw, *The Next Millionaire Next Door: Enduring Strategies for Building Wealth* (Lyons Press, 2018).
[4] Thomas J. Stanley and William D. Danko, *The Millionaire Next Door*.

Maybe you're not the one with the negative beliefs about money or your potential to earn money. We've already talked about our family's beliefs about money and how that can affect us, but maybe it runs deeper. Maybe your family actually *tells* you that you can't ever earn more money or that saving is too hard or that the economy is crappy, and you'll never be able to get ahead.

Remember that, just because someone says something to you, or about you, doesn't mean it's the truth. You do not have to own it as truth. If it contradicts who you are working toward becoming, let that garbage go. It's garbage. It's defeating and it's a lie. It's not who you are. Don't internalize it. Otherwise, you just might miss out on opportunities presented because you can't see your own greatness.

Just because in the past you may have been this or done that, it doesn't mean that is who you are today or who you will always be. The goal is to be a slightly better version of yourself than you were yesterday. Stop seeking external validation. Make *yourself* proud.

Also remember that comparison is the killer of joy, yet we do it all the time. Don't compare your journey with anyone else's. It's yours. If you have to compare yourself to anything to measure improvement, compare yourself to who you were yesterday. Each new day, aim to be a better version of yourself than who you were yesterday. Wiser, kinder, more joyful, healthier. Just because you haven't accomplished something yet doesn't mean you can't. You absolutely can!

You Just Haven't Accomplished it. . . . Yet.

I've heard it said that, if you feel that you're a failure at something (like becoming smarter about money), then you've just taken score too soon. If it's not over yet, you can't state that you've failed. As long as you're still trying, you still have a chance of winning.

Pay attention to your thoughts and self-talk that come up for you, and if they are disempowering, shift the narrative. Focus on the greatness of the outcome. I know for me, I have a lack of commitment when I am afraid of failing. That's when we need to find strength from inside, commit to deciding, and once that decision is made, our minds will start creating ways to make that decision happen. Don't allow yourself to think of the negative what-ifs, like "What if I fail?" Ask, "What great things will happen when this is a success?"

Failure Doesn't Exist if You Don't Give it Life

Failure only exists if you believe failure is a possibility, or if you quit trying. You may experience roadblocks and bumps in the road, but that doesn't mean you've failed. That means you stay persistent, get creative, and find new ways and opportunities to get to your goal.

I love to incorporate "what if's" and "why not's" into my self-talk. The next time you are considering doing something big—asking someone out on a date, applying for a job, asking for that promotion, starting the business, etc.—start engaging in self-talk about all of the positive outcomes.

What if she said yes? What if I were offered that job? What if I got that promotion? What if I started a wildly successful business? This is contrary to what your brain might usually suggest, which are all the negatives to prepare you for the hurt that will come if you hear "no" or fail at what you are trying to accomplish. Remember, your brain is there to keep you safe, which usually requires knowing what can go wrong or being "prepared for" what can go wrong—but you can start training your mind today to look for possibility and success. What you focus on expands- so focus on the positive possibilities. It may be contrary to your default mode, so it will take practice.

Also incorporate "why not" into your conversation. Why not me? Why not try? Why not ask? Why not give it a go? By removing the negatives and focusing on the possibility and positivity that might come out of the situation, you are one step closer to success in accomplishing your dreams and goals. This should encourage and inspire you! You are worthy and you are ready.

Why Not You and Why Not Now?

Throughout this book, I am going to be sharing with you lessons and takeaways that I have learned from amazing teachers. There are several books and experiences that have changed and helped reshape my life. Notice I said *re*shape. If most of what I believe to be true is engrained in my brain by age twenty-one, it's actually more challenging to reshape old thoughts, actions, and behaviors but so much more effective in creating a kick-butt life than living with the beliefs that we have always had.

Learning this next statement has literally changed my life. When I say, "I want," that means "I lack." Did you catch that?

Yes, I Want = I Lack

That punched me in the face when I first grasped that thought. I am telling the universe that I am desiring this thing that I don't have, thus lacking it in my life. Freedom from bad debt, money restraints, and scarcity thinking allows for infinite possibilities because you are no longer limited by the thoughts created by those negative feelings. This is what this work is about—removing those restrictions so you can create an empowered life with every detail designed by the limitless version of you.

Words have power, and we only want powerful words to come out of our mouths and dance around in our thoughts. Maybe restructure the statement to, "I will be/have . . ." Instead of, "I want . . ." and see what happens. Instead of saying, "I want to have $10,000 in savings towards (fill in the goal), you could say, "I will have $20,000 in savings (fill in the goal). You can make this an affirmation and focus on the objective (and ignore the negative: that you don't have it—yet).

MONEY IS ENERGY

I remember the first time I heard that saying, "Money is energy." I thought it sounded . . . fluky. So perhaps you're feeling the same way too. If you are, stay with me. It turns out many things are energy, including our emotions. Most people make purchases out of emotion, not logic. Money tends to be very emotional for a lot of people.

Some People Determine Their Self-Worth By Their Net Worth

Some people feel like they are not "enough" if they don't have flashy things to impress others and find external validation. Just like how people don't buy cars, they buy identities. Money can be someone's status symbol or money might be something that some people buy relationships with.

Money is required for the roof over our heads, the clothes on our backs, and the food in our tummies. Money is required to put gas in the car and pay our electric bill. Most vacations have a cost involved which requires... money. It's actually not about the money, it's about all of the things in our lives that money touches and affects.

Try to Imagine One Thing That Money Doesn't Touch

Money is a form of energy that we receive in exchange for contributions we make in this world. Essentially, I am trading

OUR BELIEFS ARE THE PROBLEM

my time, talents, and expertise for money. The problem, as far as I can tell, is that we can have words and actions that stop the flow of money—unintentionally, of course. Over the years of working with people making the largest financial decision of their lives (financing their homes), I have met all sorts of people with all sorts of beliefs about money. I can often identify their beliefs long before they can. Most people that I have met with have attached feelings and emotions to money. Many people live in a very self-limiting, scarcity mindset. If you would allow me to be fully transparent, this was me most of my life—scarcity mindset.

When I read the book *The Secret,* by Rhonda Byrne[5], it changed my life. I learned through that book that my thoughts become things. Through the law of attraction, I can create or basically manifest my reality. We've all been doing that our entire lives, unconsciously. But what it taught me is the power of *what* we think of. When we come from a scarcity mindset, which is unfortunately where many people are at, we focus our thoughts on the things we want or the things that we don't have. The focus should be on the things that we desire to create in our lives and the things that we are grateful for. If our focus is on the negative, we bring about more negative.

*Most People Focus on What They **Don't** Want and That's Exactly What They Get*

---
5 Rhonda Byrne, *The Secret* (Atria Books, 2018).

I want to challenge you to restructure some of your thoughts. If a regular thought of yours is, "I don't have enough money," begin to show gratitude for the money you do have and the money that is coming. You could also start saying affirmations to bring about more money. Instead of saying, "I can't afford that," you could say, "I can't afford that yet, but I will find a way to have the money to obtain my desire." I want to encourage you to read the book *The Secret*, or at least check out some of their videos on whatever search engine or streaming service you use.

Do your words attract money to you? Does money flow to you and for you? Or does it just flow through your bank account, gone before you even see it? Good energy attracts good energy. If the words you have been using about money and your beliefs about money are negative, it will keep the flow from you. Complaining, blaming, and living in a state of victimhood will repel money from you. Are you willing to give up the beliefs that others have taught you about money? Now let's learn about our mind's desires and then we will get focused on your ultimate purpose in your life.

THE WANTING MIND

I have invested a lot of time studying the psychology behind our decision-making. Most of our decision-making is unconscious to keep us safe but also satisfied. Think about a baby's behavior for just a moment. How needy is this little one?! A baby relies completely on a caretaker for their every need. When there is a need to be met, it's typically expressed through crying. Thankfully, most of us outgrow this stage. But in our mind, this same behavior can be playing out when we want something. We just can't express it the same way externally as adults—and most of us do not! But there is literally this screaming baby inside

OUR BELIEFS ARE THE PROBLEM

our mind that says, "I want this, I need this, gimme this! I must have it. If only I can have it now, it will make me so happy!"

Think about the most recent large purchase you have made. Did you desire it and think about it and research it for a long time? Or did you decide you wanted it and just satisfied that want? Most people are impulsive purchasers, even on large purchases. They want to satisfy that want, that desire, and then justify the purchase with logic after the purchase to avoid buyer's remorse.

So, when thinking about your last major purchase, how long did you allow yourself to desire or want it? Did you make a plan and save for it? Or did you just buy it, put it on a credit card, or get a loan for it, and figure out the details later? Most people are completely unaware of the "wanting mind." However, it can literally rule your life and keep you from your ultimate bigger goals. When you desire something beyond your basic needs and it's all you can think about, your mind tricks you into believing that if you just satisfy that want then you will be happy. I can recall many times in my life like this. It was a new purse, a new car, a new phone. The list could go on and on for many pages. But once I discovered the wanting mind—once I was aware that it was ruling me—I was actually able to make some big shifts in my life.

I'm not saying there's anything wrong with wanting things. We all want things. But what I have learned through my studies is that the parts of your brain that get excited and lit up when you want something are actually more active in the process of wanting than when you actually satisfy that want. To say it another way, when you satisfy that want, it's actually not as satisfying as the desire for that thing. So, once you have it, you will literally find something new to desire and the cycle starts all over again. Lurking behind every want is another want (that will be revealed or created once you fill the current want), just prowling and lingering. It will be a never-ending list of wants. Start noticing those you are close to in your life. You might start noticing there are a lot of people walking around clamoring about what they want. When I started noticing this, I almost started sounding like a toddler demanding, "Mine! Mine!" for everything in her little life. I don't care to sound like that, so I am upgrading my words.

That thing you desire will not bring you the happiness you think it will. When we understand that we will always want for something to bring fulfillment and happiness, but it may not fulfill us the way we are hoping for, then we can reign back those emotions a little bit. I used to think I needed to satisfy that want immediately. And unfortunately, that is exactly the behavior that got me into really high credit card debt and had me justifying an enormous car loan and monthly payment. If you can see how some of your past behaviors are due to your wanting mind, then let's create a plan to keep it in check. We have to prioritize and separate needs from wants. Needs get met, wants may get fulfilled, but it could put you in a financial rut.

> **Money is a tool to help you live your life with purpose**

We know we live in a world where we don't have to wait for a thing. Everything can be delivered to our door within a matter of days—if not hours—or instantly electronically. I want to share some remarkable research that was done all the way back in the 1960s (published in the 1970s). When I heard of

OUR BELIEFS ARE THE PROBLEM

this study, it really fascinated me. This experiment is known as "The Marshmallow Test" and it was pioneered by Walter Mischel. And since then, there has been a lot of research that dives into the power of delayed gratification. Picture a four-or five-year-old who is ushered into a room with a two-way mirror. This unsuspecting kid is invited to sit at a table where a delicious, fresh, jumbo marshmallow is awaiting. The child is told that this is his or her marshmallow to enjoy, but if the child can wait "a few minutes" to gobble up the marshmallow until the adult returns, they can have a second marshmallow. Think of the challenge this sweet young child is experiencing! Imagine waiting for as long as fifteen minutes for the researcher to return. Enjoy one now, or two a little later? There was so much emotion and attempt at restraint—it's truly worth looking into more deeply on your own. A quick web search will show you a slew of really cute videos of very young children faced with the dilemma of instant gratification or demonstrating self-control for even more to enjoy! You'll see them fidgeting, touching, smelling, and even licking the sweet treat. I just went onto YouTube to watch a few minutes of one of the videos. It will make you smile, if not laugh! Check it out now just so you get a true picture of what I am describing. Isn't that a great representation of many of the financial choices in our lives?

What would you do? I would have fallen face-first into that marshmallow in no time! But wait—for what? I would have been willing to enjoy it right away and then . . . punish myself for not having a second one to enjoy because I had no self-control. And then internally I would feel lousy because of my lack of ability to restrain my overwhelming emotions and need to satisfy my wants. What would you have done? What you tend to do now is what we likely would have done as a child.

FINISH FINANCIALLY FREE

We humans have a tendency to want what we want, now. Especially since the future can be so unpredictable. Let's do our own experiment. Let's say I was going to offer you one hundred dollars today or $120 in two weeks. Since we know today is certain and two weeks could feel like a long time from now, we tend to discount our financial future. The majority of people will opt for the one hundred dollars today. We want shorter time and quicker satisfaction to avoid waiting longer or later, even if there is more to be had or to gain in the future. To our own detriment, we can't wait for it. Just like those little five-year-olds.

Here is what is most fascinating to me about that marshmallow experiment—they followed these kiddos, for forty years!!! The researchers tracked many different areas of the lives of those children as they went from school age into adulthood. What they discovered is incredible—for me, it was shocking and eye-opening.

Those kiddos who were able to demonstrate delayed gratification (let's not forget, this is incredible self-control) scored higher on their SATs, had lower rates of substance abuse, had better social skills, and overall had higher measures on other life metrics such as lower divorce rates, lower likelihood of obesity, and higher performing jobs. When you think about it, breaking down each of these outcomes, it makes sense. Demonstrating that kind of self-control is often what is needed when faced with peer pressure. We need to commit to things that can be challenging and often don't have instant outcomes (such as educational goals, working through marital ups and downs, and working out to lose weight or maintain a healthy lifestyle).

This brought me to a question that perhaps you, too, are left with—is this ability to demonstrate delayed gratification and self-control something that one is born with or is it a learned skill? I believe it can be developed and strengthened with the right habits in place and proper goals as the focus. Self-control is an essential life skill, and when engaged, can help create an overall more kick-butt life.

SELF-CONTROL
Tony Robbins, one of my favorite mentors, lays out a four-step process to develop self-control. First, start small. Create a goal so easy you can't fail. And next time, improve by 1 percent and you will watch your confidence grow with each small goal achieved. Second, make rules. On his website, he uses the example of waiting three days before allowing yourself to make a major purchase as a rule. Or a rule of "if you've spent more than five minutes debating a purchase, you don't need it." Step three, practice gratitude. I love that this is in here. Gratitude is the key to so many blessings life has to offer and having gratitude for the things we already have can help delay instant wants. Being grateful for the clothes and car you already have helps us appreciate what we have and helps us see the difference between a want and a need. We already have all we need. It's usually a want we are chasing after. And fourth, remind yourself of your goals.

Whatever your big goal is, keep that in the forefront of your mind when it comes time to make decisions about saving and spending. For example, I love to travel the world. But the kind of travel we enjoy several times a year is planned and paid for, because I practice delayed gratification. Believe me, I lust after a few cars I see on the road, but my perfectly fine-driving seven-year-old sedan that is paid off is my key to having a vacation fund. I can put $500 a month towards our amazing adventures because I don't finance a new car. There is a trade-off and pay-off for every decision we make.

Tony Robbins had it right. Without starting small, making rules, practicing gratitude, and reminding yourself of your goals, you simply can't develop self-control.

PURPOSE

Before we can get into the second section of the book where I begin to teach about spending, saving, foundational finance, and credit, we have to know our purpose for our life. Isn't this the question we are all really asking: What is the purpose of my life?

What is purpose? One definition of purpose is the reason for which something (or someone) was created or exists. It's from this definition of purpose that I'd like to focus on. God created only one you. You are fearfully and wonderfully made, and I believe part of our journey here is not to *find* our purpose but to *create* it, and through that creation we can discover what really lights us up. When it aligns with your soul, every part of your being should feel elated. Your purpose isn't going to be found in just one thing; it's going to be found in all the things that you do and give and share.

Money is a tool to help you live your life with purpose. For me, I intentionally learn every day so that I can continue growing. Sometimes that involves reading or getting coaching and sometimes that involves going to a seminar or participating in an education course. The more I grow, the more purpose I feel building in my life. I tend to make decisions with more intentionality.

CREATE A PLAN

It's important to create a plan for where you'd like to be in one year, three years, and five years. It's also important to envision what your later years will look like. I am at the age now that I need to think about what my life will look like ten years from now. Am I the boss of my schedule or will my schedule rule my life? Do I have freedom in what I purchase and where I get to travel? Do I have my money working for me or am I working for my money? When I first started thinking about the word *retirement*, I would think about old people in rocking chairs just wasting the day away. There isn't much purpose in life at that point, is there? So, the thought of retirement turned me off. Not because I didn't think I'd have the money to fund my retirement but because I didn't want to stop. I have been able to create a new definition for myself and so I want to encourage you to think about what later in life looks like for you. For me, my older years means getting to choose what I spend my time on. I will likely never stop working because I do believe it will keep me young, but I won't have to take on the jobs or clients that don't bring me fulfillment and joy. I will get to travel on vacation without being attached to my computer and my e-mail. If I want to spend a week in the mountains and then a month at the beach, I can do that! Changing how I viewed "retirement" actually helped expand my purpose, because my reasons for getting up every day, hustling, and using my money to have an awesome life and also bless others will continue through those golden years. I am excited for you to create your plan, too!

Consider something with me. This next teaching is from *Landmark Education®*. *Landmark Education* is a powerful personal development program that creates radical transformation in your thinking and thus, your life. There are so many amazing things that I learned through their seminars, but I want to share this one takeaway with you now. There are things you know. There are things you think you know. There are things you don't know. And there are things you don't know that you don't know. How much of the world's information to be known do you think you know? A tiny dot, right? A speckle of a piece of dust of all there is to know. When we hold on to the thoughts that we already know, it prohibits our minds from being open to learning new things or a new perspective about things. Sometimes we believe we know something to be true, but it was a poor belief of the past or a skewed way to look at it that is actually keeping us stuck. We don't know what we don't know. I know it just sounds like, "Yeah, I don't know everything," but I want you to consider letting go of all of your beliefs about who you are, who you were, what you have or don't have, and what you can and will have or won't have, because those beliefs, even bigger than your money beliefs, are the stories that play in your subconscious and may silently sabotage what's possible for you and your life.

You Don't Know What You Don't Know

Let this statement free you so that you may now be curious and open to learning, exploring, and abundantly growing with knowledge that will reshape your destiny. Most people will never stop long enough to examine their beliefs. It causes so many people to just meander through life and try to figure it

OUR BELIEFS ARE THE PROBLEM

out as they go along, unable to understand why they can't get ahead. It's easy to just bump along on the road and not put in the hard work of examining what is working and not working in our beliefs, habits, and behaviors. Our environments have conditioned us this way, to just go along with what we think we believe. We live as though we are subject to these assumptions we made and treat it as reality.

Before we move to the next chapter, would you consider doing something seriously cheesy? I mean, *really* cheesy? It's an exercise that will have you rolling your eyes but might turn out to be highly effective in getting your mind to start thinking about the future, which is difficult to do when we can barely get through this week and this month.

I want to challenge you right now to stop for a moment, grab a pen and a piece of paper and write a letter to your future self. I did this at a seminar once and had all sorts of (judgmental) thoughts about it. But in the end, it actually changed my thought process enough that I saw a new light shed on what was possible, so I want to share this with you, too. In her kick-butt book, *You Are a Badass at Making Money*[6], Jen Sincero also suggests this. Maybe she and I were at the same seminar? Anyway, you are going to write a letter to your future self, the version of you that is living freely and living your actual dreams. Tell your future self your current feelings and fears (*this is hard, I am nervous, I hate being in debt, I can't wait to live my dream*). What does it feel like today; the way things are in this moment? How does that compare to where you desire to be? Now shift to writing about what you are desiring and creating for your future. How do you envision your relationship with money once you have gone through this work? What are you most hopeful

---

6   Jen Sincero, You Are a Badass at Making Money: Master the Mindset of Wealth (New York: Viking, 2018).

for in the future? What excites you the most? What will it feel like to accomplish those goals?

I truly believe that once you spend a few minutes feeling the feelings and experiencing what you think it will feel like, you will actually experience the emotions tied to it all. You will feel the energy in your body, and it will help move you toward your goals.

It's my hope that you will be open to new empowering beliefs and replace some of your words, and especially your inner talk, to propel you towards who you are working to become. Now... smile. Let's get curious.

CHAPTER 3

HABITS WE HAVE FORMED

Have you ever noticed we are creatures of habit? The older I get, the more I find myself just going through the motions. I suppose I always have. We often drive to work, the gym, or friends' homes the same way, have the same routine at the end of the day, and go to the same restaurants and stores. Our actions become second nature—one less thing to have to think about. It's just easy.

The reason we need to start here with habits before diving into our finances is because for many of us, a habit (or two) is ruling our minds and our lives. And once you can take ownership and overcome that habit, you are proving to yourself just how strong you are and finding possibility and hope for being the designer of your life. Sometimes one or two habits can keep us from seeing what's possible for true joy and fulfillment. We get what we *think* we deserve. So, elevate your thoughts—you are worthy! You deserve great things, so work for them and allow them to flow to you. Here is another thought to ponder: Do you allow certain things to show up that don't align with your goals?

We Get What We Tolerate

There was a time in my life I felt so very trapped as a result of my decisions. I just felt stuck. How did I end up here? I asked myself that question pretty much every day. But I found all I was doing was focusing on all the bad choices that led me to what felt like a deadbeat life. I needed to reframe the questions. I needed to ask, what do I want for my life and what's possible? Some of my habits actually made me feel like a slave. I had to overcome a few to prove I could do it instead of doing what I was always doing, which was proving myself defeated and ruled by the habit.

During the pandemic I was working extremely long days most days of the week. My work is very thought-intensive and by the end of the day, I am just wiped out. Not being able to live life as we once knew it, I found myself having a drink, or several, at the end of every day. It was how I announced to my brain that work was complete for the day, and I had permission to check out for the night. And we would just watch something on some streaming device. Habit. It became comfortable, but not healthy. Drinking every night is not something that is easy to admit. I didn't love being reliant on something to help my brain shut down from work mode. It became habit. We cannot live life on our own terms if habits and familiarity rule the mind. I want to be a master of my life, not a slave to the habits that I have allowed to take over my life.

What part of your life is habit but may not be serving you well?

Here is a non-exhaustive list, just to get your mind thinking about what present habit(s) might exist that may be hindering your goals:

- » Caffeine
- » Alcohol
- » Spending money out of habit (such as a daily fix of _____)
- » Therapy shopping or impulse spending
- » An unhealthy relationship
- » Dipping/chewing
- » Vaping/smoking
- » Biting your nails
- » Snacking at 9:00 pm
- » Hitting the snooze button
- » Procrastination
- » Spending too many hours a day gaming/streaming/on social media
- » Not following through on commitments
- » Nervous movement (like tapping, shaking your foot, or clicking a pen)

You get the idea. Not necessarily all *bad* but may be uninspiring and detracting from improving your self-esteem. The reason I even bring this up is because I see a lot of people who spend money a certain way, who stay in jobs for longer than they should, or use (fill in the blank) as a reason or excuse as to why they are where they are. Sometimes we need to replace a bad habit (or three!) in order to show up as our best selves in other aspects of our lives.

FINISH FINANCIALLY FREE

I just want to bring to your awareness that the habits we have created, tolerated, and still allow in our lives shape who we are in this moment. But it doesn't have to remain that way. If I could be really vulnerable right now, outside of the dipping/chewing on that list, I was pretty much the puppet of all of those habits. I just didn't see them as habits. I didn't really see them at all. I was not aware of any of them.

It usually takes someone saying something, having a bad experience, or some reason worth changing for in order for us to even acknowledge our habits and then make positive moves to conquer them and upgrade to a self-improving habit. Only when we create new habits can we propel forward in goal-getting actions.

I stopped drinking coffee for months and months just to prove to myself that I could in fact live and function without it (some of you just lost your mind at that thought). I still drink coffee, but it just doesn't control my mornings anymore. I smoked cigarettes from ages thirteen to thirty and quit—one of the proudest accomplishments of my life. That shit isn't easy to quit!

I have found that I stayed in many of my habits because I simply tolerated them. Once you begin to identify some of your habits, you must then figure out what to do about them. You may need to ask those closest in your life to help you see your habits. I literally had no idea I was chewing my nails incessantly. Well, let me rephrase that sentence. I was well *aware* that I would chew my nails down to the point of bleeding, until there was nothing left to chew on but skin. And the next day my fingertips would hurt, even to type. Yet I continued. It wasn't until I got married that my husband would tell me nearly every night, "Stop chewing. Stop chewing your nails. You're doing it again." I was forced to find a solution. My habit was affecting someone I cared about. Just like when I quit smoking, I had to find resources, distractions, and something to keep me from continuing the habit.

I finally stopped biting my nails by coating them with gel nail polish. I remember someone telling me a story about a salesperson who was crushing a sales presentation and ready to "close the sale" when the buyer noticed his nails. She asked what was up with his nails. It turns out, he chews them (just like I had!) down to where they bled and hurt. The buyer refused to close the sale saying that she couldn't work with someone who had no self-control. Shocking, right?

I was a little ticked off and a little embarrassed when I heard that story. But I didn't want to feel that way, and I certainly didn't want to demonstrate the inability to have self-control. But being fully transparent, I *couldn't* control chewing my nails without the resource I sought out. We can always find a way, if we are willing, to overcome the things that may seem to rule us. But first we have to **see** the daily habits that make up our routines. I have heard the following before—I think it was from Tony Robbins—but it applies here:

"If You Keep Doing What You've Always Done, You'll Keep Getting What You've Always Gotten"

For the record, I have found that you can't just stop a habit. You have to replace it with a different routine or healthy habit.

FINISH FINANCIALLY FREE

Some financial habits you can watch for are spending money out of boredom or when you are feeling sad, or the daily drive-thru for your six-dollar caffeine fix. I suggest you start with just a few. And I'm certainly not suggesting you have a long list of bad habits. But in case you have several, just start with one or two.

Here are some steps to make stopping a bad habit easier.

STEP 1: List out the habit or habits you'd like to address. Pick out the one that you think would have the most radical change in your life if it were eliminated and then replaced. Focus on that habit specifically for this exercise. Then you can repeat the process in the future for your next habit to tackle.

STEP 2: Write out as many reasons and excuses that you can come up with as to why you have tolerated this action or behavior. And don't just stop at one or two reasons. If you're anything like me, you could come up with fifty excuses to justify the habit. When it came to smoking, it was my crutch and calming agent. It's how I signify to my brain that my meal was over, it's what I did when I enjoyed an adult beverage, it was my excuse to walk away from work and take a break for a few minutes. It became a lot of things for me. So don't be surprised if you come up with a long list of reasons and justifications for your habit. You may also find these reasons and excuses are what have prevented you from creating an extraordinary life. Some of my excuses included lacking the drive to change it and lacking the courage to try.

> **We get what we think we deserve**

HABITS WE HAVE FORMED

STEP 3: Let's identify what you will gain by keeping this habit. And then let's flip the question and ask what you might gain if you stop this habit. What I found to be interesting when I worked through this exercise was that there were plenty of things that were tangible if I quit smoking such as saving money, improving my health, and smelling better. What surprised me was that my list was even longer for the intangibles, such as a sense of pride for accomplishing breaking the stronghold of a habit. I guess I didn't realize how much it controlled me and now I can control it.

A similar thing happened when I realized I would go shopping out of boredom. When I had "nothing better to do," I would find myself browsing through a home decor store or a discount clothing store looking at dresses. I can assure you, I don't need another trinket on the shelf or one more dress. When I learned that this was a default habit to kill some time (and money I didn't have to just spend), I eliminated that behavior. That action alone of not walking into one of those stores just to "kill time" saved me well over one hundred dollars a month! It just wasn't even in my awareness until I took the time to look at my habits. Now it's your turn.

*Habits I would love to drop that if could expel from my life would have a positive impact in my life:*_____

_____
_____
_____
_____
_____
_____
_____

FINISH FINANCIALLY FREE

The one that hurts the most with the biggest negative impact is:

_____

_____

Take a few minutes and just jot down some habits. I want to encourage you to tackle the first one or two habits you'd like to see conquered in your life, come back, and see what else you might be able to accomplish by intentionally taking control. Momentum builds from momentum. But don't try to take on too many changes at one time. Once you have accomplished taking control of that first habit, then consider taking on the next one.

I realize many of your habits you have listed and will tackle may not be (directly) affiliated with money, such as therapy shopping. But you may find that the habit or two you acknowledge and replace may cost you in time and money, such as vaping, alcohol, or a daily $6 frappe trip. Even habits that have nothing to do with spending money directly, such as biting your nails, could cost you in other ways, such as that example of the salesperson who lost the sale. Ever stop to notice that "bad" habits are something we just kind of . . . fall into, while "good" habits seem like work to accomplish (working out, going to bed at a decent time to get enough sleep, eating healthy, or getting to work on time)? There is an effective way to incorporate new "good" habits into your life. It's called habit stacking. I learned about this from Dr. BJ Fogg in his book *Tiny Habits*[7]. It's a great book for creating a plan to change habits (and I also recommend *Atomic Habits* by James Clear[8]. Both amazing and life-altering books!).

---

[7] B. J. Fogg, *Tiny Habits: The Small Changes That Change Everything* (Boston: Houghton Mifflin Harcourt, 2020).
[8] James Clear, *Atomic Habits: Tiny Changes, Remarkable Results: An Easy and Proven Way to Build Good Habits and Break Bad Ones* (London: Cornerstone press, 2022).

Habit stacking is associating a new habit you would like to incorporate in your life and connecting it with an existing habit. If you want to get in the habit of incorporating vitamins or supplements into your daily routine but keep "forgetting" to take them, associate it with your daily morning coffee or brushing your teeth. Have the vitamins right there, next to your coffee maker or your toothbrush, and every time you make your morning coffee, you take your vitamins. I enjoy watching videos on social media but found it was eating up a lot of my time (becoming a bad habit), because of how much time I spent there. And I hate getting on my stepper machine but I really need to. I can habit stack these two by allowing myself to watch the videos only while I am on the stepper. It motivates me to get on the stepper because I get to enjoy the videos for a designated amount of time.

So, let's say you have a habit of procrastinating paying your bills, which often results in late fees and potential late payments reflecting on your credit report, which negatively affects your credit score and profile. Perhaps you can habitually stack your payday with specific bills being paid first, before spending money on groceries, going out, or treating yourself. You likely jump into your bank app on payday to see what your current balance is. While you are in your bank app, immediately pay the bills that are due that pay cycle. If you align your payday with bill pay, as in the same exact day, you will be creating a new habit, and more importantly replacing an old story and belief that you cannot pay bills on time. You absolutely can and will be proving it to yourself! Procrastination is often a symptom of fear. Perhaps you feared not being able to pay all your bills, and so you avoided paying (all or some of) them. By aligning it with payday before any money is spent on the weekend, at the mall, or on groceries, you can prove it can be paid on time and avoid the extra fees and negative feelings. It will feel so rewarding as you are proving to yourself you are able, capable, and actually doing it!

Getting back to the habit or habits you want to dominate and replace, what can you incorporate into your life to replace that bad habit and increase the likelihood it will become a good habit by stacking it with an existing habit? Our routines are habit, so start noticing your actions and patterns in your daily life and notice where in your routine you can stack the new habit.

Some habits will require the help of others. I tried at least twenty different ways to quit smoking. I finally found the way that worked for me, but I certainly wasn't able to do it myself. I tried everything from patches to hypnosis to acupuncture. You may have to hire a professional to conquer your bad habit. The way I see it, if you've identified a bad habit that seems to be ruling your life and you want it gone, you can either address it now or you can be in the same place in a couple of years from now. Let's make the decision to conquer this once and for all! Free yourself from this habit.

Get it Gone!

Steven Covey wrote a well-known book called *7 Habits of Highly Effective People*[9]. The first three of the seven habits

---

[9] Stephen R. Covey, James Charles Collins, and Sean Covey, *The 7 Habits of Highly Effective People: Powerful Lessons in Personal Change* (London: Simon&Schuster, 2020).

are referred to as self-mastery habits. I want to share my biggest takeaways from these first three habits. As mentioned earlier, we can't just break a habit, we have to replace it. And the first three of the seven habits he lists are the keys we need to make this work!

First, Mr. Covey says to be proactive in our thoughts and actions. So many people focus on the things outside of their control, complain about those things, and focus on their circumstances (which are often a result of their own decisions). Instead, focus on your inner self and your character. Instead, you should focus on your attitude, educational skills, enthusiasm about life, and your mood. These things make you proactive instead of reactive to those outside things you can't control. Although we may not be able to control those outside factors, we can control how we respond to them and life situations. If you want to be ahead of almost everyone else, don't focus on "looking good" like the majority of people do—focus on having incredible character and becoming an awesome person that takes action instead of complaining and wallowing in your lousy mood without doing anything to improve yourself.

The second habit he speaks of is to begin with the end in mind. What the heck? You may be thinking, "I can barely make it to the end of the week, and you want me to think of 'the end?'" Yes. Don't check out, this is actually really good. He says that everything is created twice, first in your mind, and then it shows up in your life. If you don't know what your actual target is, then you will just wander. And I don't mean the cute, "not all who wander are lost" mantra, because Lord knows we like to venture off and wander. But have an overarching goal when you start something. Decide what you want to tackle. Where do you want to be with specific goals and also where do you want to see yourself in your life three, five, or ten years from now?

Have you ever gone back to your high school yearbook to the page where you wrote where you see yourself at the (old) age of thirty? I wrote that I was going to be blissfully married (and of course, he was super hot, by the way) to a chiropractor with two kids, a golden retriever, and a BMW that I drive to work but a Jeep Wrangler for weekend beach trips. I am loaded with cash, not stressed about my very successful career, and planning my next international vacation.

Do you want to know what my life was *really* like when I was thirty? I was divorced because I settled for someone who was not at all who I should have married, and I was broke *and* poor. My financial world was crumbling, and I was basically out of work and going back to college to get another degree so I didn't have to feel the way I was feeling about my life in that moment—you know—to create more "security." I had recently broken off my engagement, I was drinking way too much, and stupidly dabbling in drugs to mask how unhappy I was in my life. Whew. That was a mouthful. It was pretty much the complete opposite of where I saw my life at that age. I just *knew* at the age of eighteen I was going to kick ass for twelve years and then be at some happy place that likely doesn't exist for most thirty-year-olds. Most thirty-year-olds are trying to pay off college and credit card debt, likely in a relationship (or like some of us, in and out and in and out of relationships, praying this next one is *the* one), and considering home ownership. Or maybe a puppy. Tough choices abound and you are just trying to figure out this whole adult thing.

"The Best Way to Predict Your Future is to Create it"
—Steven Covey

So, back to beginning with the end in mind. I know my end game, but it took me a few decades to figure it out. Now, I know I don't want to work until age seventy-six like my mom had to. I know I want to travel the world sooner rather than later because I don't want my arthritic eighty-year-old knees and oxygen tank to get in the way of me rocking out in Greece. Gotta get there soon, not as a great grandma! That means I have to have a plan that includes money for me to travel now and each year while I am young enough to get around and to have enough created (notice I didn't say saved in a retirement account) for me to smash my goals. I want to quit from "have to work" at age fifty-five. And that means I get to be selective of who I take on as clients, take Fridays off here and there, and leave my email inbox madness at 4:00 pm every day if I want (instead of working the current hellacious hours I currently am and feeling like projects and new assignments rule my time)—it will be my choice! I also have plans to take an international trip and incredible stateside vacation every year to empty our bucket list before we are too old to enjoy it all. I know how much to contribute each year towards the travel fund, and I know my goal for assets and net worth for when I turn fifty-five. I have a plan. *Now* I know what to do. How many people can say that?

Do you want to be able to say that? It's not difficult to execute, but most won't. It's simple, but not easy. And it is a lot like anything in life; some days are better than others in accomplishing my goals. So how do we make this happen? Through habit three, of course!

Steven Covey's third habit is to put first things first: prioritize. This can be difficult for me, so I am going to guess it might be difficult for you, too. When several things feel like priority, how do you determine which one comes first? This is going to sound cheesy, but sometimes I take myself out of the situation and try to look at it like I am a medical professional diagnosing the problem. There are all sorts of symptoms, but usually one (occasionally two) causes of those symptoms. Ask yourself, what hurts the worst? Is it having 25 percent of your take-home pay going to pay off debts? Then get it gone. Start there. Perhaps that is the priority over saving. Once you feel a little relief from the balances going down and you can breathe a little, then think about moving money into savings.

The very first step in the action plan will be uncovering your money story. Then you are going to conquer replacing one or two (bad) habits in your life that are keeping you held back, stuck, and distracted. It's time to start picturing your kick-butt life, which is probably not possible if you procrastinate, watch five hours a night of shows, or scroll through social media, and have no plan created.

> **Pay attention to your thoughts and self-talk that come up for you and if they are disempowering, shift the narrative**

I have accomplished incredibly huge goals in my life, but it all started with one distinct principle: decision. I made a decision to no longer live in indecision. I learned this principle when I first read *Think and Grow Rich* by Napoleon Hill[10]. It is one of the most impactful and influential books I have ever read. To go from a life of consumption to contribution, it takes decision. I made a decision about what I wanted my life to look like: what kind of house I lived in, what kind of car I drove, the travel we experienced every year, all the way down to what shoes were in the closet. Once I had that visual, I knew I had to decide what it was going to take to get there. Working three jobs for crappy pay was not going to get me that life. Maybe if I borrowed my way to it all, but then I would be working only to pay debt payments. Not the life for me. In the moment of that decision, I felt empowered to start making the adjustments to create that kind of life. Decision. Decide.

"In Our Moment of Decision Our Destiny is Created"
—Tony Robbins

SIDE NOTE: when Napoleon Hill in *Think and Grow Rich* speaks of "money," I replace it with the word "impact" in my mind. Yes, I want money—but not for the purpose of accumulating money—rather, I want money for the impact I can make in this world with it.

What if what you believed to be "money issues" turned out to be inaccurate beliefs and a bad habit (or several habits)? Would getting in action to replace those habits change the

---

10 Napoleon Hill, *Think and Grow Rich* (United States: Fortune Publishing Group, 2013).

financial trajectory of this month, this year, and your life? What habits do you need to change in your life to live life on your terms? Just know the old habits are going to create resistance, because they are comfortable living with you and don't want to get kicked out. I truly believe that happiness is being in control of your own life. When you can prove to yourself that you can conquer bad habits and create great habits, those actions and behaviors will help shape the exact life you want for yourself. And that is exactly what you have been focused on in this chapter. I want to applaud you for identifying the big habit that is ruling a lot of your life to work on replacing with a good habit—stacked of course! That habit may be costing you in more ways than you have acknowledged in the past. Often, dropping that one big bad habit can clear the space for all sorts of amazing things to open up for you, even above and beyond money saved by dropping the habit. You might even begin to feel anxiety and stress levels go down. Once you master defeating a bad habit and replacing it with a good one in your overall life, you will be able to prove to yourself you can do it. This will help pave the way for success in your financial life once you start creating healthy financial habits, which we will learn about later in the book. Your amazing life and big dreams are waiting for you to start creating and exploring!

Give Yourself Permission to Get Exactly What You Want Out of Life!

CHAPTER 4

COUPLES AND MONEY

I can't help but think of all the television shows that shaped my mind growing up. There were many shows that displayed a couple, each with their own strong personality traits and quirky behaviors, often for entertainment purposes. I think about *Married...With Children, Everybody Loves Raymond, Modern Family*, and even cartoons like *Family Guy* and *The Simpsons*. They taught us a lot about relationships—both *what* to do and what *not* to do! Usually, the couples were complete opposites of each other and would really struggle through some of life's challenges, usually creating laughs for us and often leaving us shaking our heads (probably thinking, "Glad that's not my plus one!"). They often didn't talk about the difficult things. Poor Al Bundy is forced to work a job he hates selling shoes and when it is payday, his kids and wife suddenly "love him" for a fleeting moment. I am sure there are plenty of moments we watched that reflect the challenges of life a couple has to face and figure out together but often from opposite perspectives.

> **I believe that people don't fight about money. I believe they fight about the use of money, where it goes, and how it is spent and saved**

Have you ever wondered why it is so hard for couples to talk about money? If you look up the top reasons for divorce and conflict in relationships, it's usually over money, in marriage and in business relationships. So why is this? Let's go back to the very first principle we covered which is our beliefs about money. Most of us have never questioned it and we've just rolled with the motions as long as we can remember. Since we are a product of our environment and the beliefs that are instilled in us by others, it feels like second nature and just the way things are. But consider that because of your experiences, you have a bias toward what you believe to be as truth. And so does your significant other. If we don't know what our beliefs are and where our beliefs come from, how can we possibly have a conversation about them?

Hence, we have awkwardness and discomfort and angst when financial problems show up. How do we talk about something we don't know or understand? And how can you possibly defend what you believe when you're not even sure about *what* you believe about money? You're left with defending behaviors and habits and actions which likely haven't been serving you very well. Even if you are a saver, it might be at the cost of enjoying your hard-earned money.

I believe that people don't fight about money. I believe they fight about the use of money, where it goes, and how it is spent and saved. About seventy to 75 percent of couples are money opposites. It makes good sense—if you have two spenders, they will be claiming bankruptcy every seven years. So that spender needs the balance of a saver, but if you are opposites in your relationship with money, and add to that your warped beliefs about money, now enters the disagreements and fights. It's not that we don't necessarily understand money, we don't understand our beliefs about and relationship with money, because it's just always been . . . the way you handled it. Unquestioned beliefs that rule big decisions in your life are impossible to defend or explain in a conversation, wouldn't you agree?

If you have a significant other in your life, make sure you each do the work in chapter two to uncover your individual beliefs. And then share it with each other. I truly believe the number one reason why couples can't get on the same page with money is because individually, they don't know their own money beliefs. And then mix in another belief system, which is likely unknown, and voila! It's a recipe for disputes, fights, disagreements about how and where money is spent, and possibly money infidelity. What the heck does that mean? I have seen where couples don't know how their partner is using their money. There are secrets or even lies about how and where money is spent.

Every relationship is unique, so I can't tell you if you should have a shared bank account or separate bank accounts, but I will tell you to talk about it. What works for my husband and me is that we know how much goes to our bills, and he contributes his portion from his income. I have seen some couples split the bills 50/50 and put it into a shared account that pays the bills, or they correlate their income to their "share" of contribution.

FINISH FINANCIALLY FREE

If one of you earns $5,000 a month and the other $3,500, perhaps you split the contribution with the equal percentage. The higher wage earner pays 60 percent of the amount owed, and the other contributes 40 percent of the amount owed. Some people split the bills; you pay housing, utilities, and insurance, and I will pay car payments, food costs, and credit card bills. At least talk about it! And then check in once a month to make sure everything has been paid on time and discuss what is left to tackle. I do recommend having a checking account (again whether it is solo or joint is up to you two) for bills and a savings account for storing towards goals such as buying a home, a business, travel, etc that has intentional and structured deposits into it that you both can agree on.

So discuss how you will handle the necessities—the actual cost of living (housing, food, insurance, etc.), split or shared in a way that makes sense for you as a couple and you both can agree on. What about credit card or student loan debt? Car payments and spending habits? Hobbies and habits? Some couples say, "What is yours is yours to take care of and pay off." Some couples go all in together and tackle the debt as a joint venture. Have a conversation and make sure the conversation doesn't shame one of you if you have brought a lot of past debt into the situation. The conversation should be honoring to each of you and result in a plan to tackle what you are facing each month. You said YES when you merged your lives, so let's create a conversation around how it gets handled.

Ignoring debt or past collections won't help your bigger goals towards an excellent credit score. A great credit score will help you to not overpay in interest charges when you do go to borrow for things like a car or financing your home purchase. If one of you has a checkered past and needs to clean up some prior mistakes, talk about it. Don't try to hide it or cover it up. Keeping it from your partner is just going to make things more difficult in the future when it comes up, as it will eventually come up. Your partner loves you, and just because you have some debts to pay off or collection accounts, it doesn't change how they feel about you. It won't change their love for you! But keeping information a secret or just not being fully transparent can create doubt about being able to trust you. If you don't have trust, it can weaken or hurt the relationship. Let's not keep these things hidden out of fear of what your partner is going to think. You trust each other with emotional and physical intimacy, so you will need to get to the place where you can trust each other with money.

Set up a time where the two of you can have a private and open conversation in a safe place, like at home, just the two of you—no accusations, no putting the other person down. Just sharing the reality of your current financial situation: your debts, your budget to show your current spending (if this is not shared already), and what troubles you about your personal situation. I hated having credit card debt. It hurt. I hated the monthly payments, the interest I was throwing money at, and the thousands of dollars hanging over my head. It felt like it was pulling me down by the ankles and keeping me from saving towards fun and big goals, even stopping me from buying a home. That feels lousy, and it was truly difficult to talk about. I put a label on myself for it and it took a toll on my self-esteem. It limited me from what I actually wanted out of life.

Just make sure the words you are using when talking about debts and financial obligations are not disempowering to your partner. Kindness, consideration, and patience are going to be key here. Remember you both have different experiences and relationships with money. I have also learned that we tend to move through time and space at different speeds than one another. So, it might take a little extra time for your partner to come around to the spending plan, negotiating spending and savings, and coming to terms with the new plans. Acknowledge that they likely already feel lousy about prior behaviors with debt and spending. But creating a plan to tackle it **together** is the first step to feeling the freedom that this plan will create.

> **This is not the time to be critical or judgmental. It's time to put it all out there.**

So how do we set up a plan to reduce the stress, anxiety, and fights around money? Carefully—that's how! Everyone handles stressful things differently. Stress often incites the fight, flight, or freeze situation to occur. I know when I am facing a stressful situation, all I want to do is recoil and go hide. I don't like to face it; I freeze. I procrastinate and hide from it as long as possible. If that is you, I understand. Not everyone can tackle things head-on, so consider that this may be even more difficult for your partner than it is for you and tell them it's difficult for you to work through as well. This is going to kick up a lot of emotions, and a lot of emotions are tied to old beliefs. You may hear yourself saying words like, "I don't want to . . . I shouldn't have to . . . I don't do numbers . . . I can't figure this stuff out . . . " Those are all to keep you from having to experience or feel the emotions those old beliefs are going to conjure up.

Remember, many people have these beliefs: "There is never enough money," "There's no way to get ahead," "If I want something, I deserve to have it," "Money is evil," "I'm scared to look at my numbers," "I could be successful with money if it weren't for _____," "I have never been good with numbers," "It will all work out in the end . . ."

This is not the time to be critical or judgmental. It's time to put it all out there. Share your budgets/spending plan and your list of outstanding debts (with the current outstanding balance, monthly payment, and interest rate). This is the time to acknowledge what the budget shows as your numbers and compare the outflow to the inflow. It's vitally important to see just how much you (may) come up short each month, so you know where to start. If it's $500 a month, see if you can go back and forth and agree where you can cut back on spending. It might be as simple as cutting a few luxury items out of your spending for a designated amount of time until you get to a place where the debt is paid off or there is a little padding in the bank account after everything is paid.

I read a book by Ruth L. Hayden called *For Richer, Not Poorer*[11]. It's an older book but has some great wisdom in there for couples to start their money conversations and tackle their differences and money issues. Ruth recommends having a weekly money meeting. Every week, it is a designated, uninterrupted time together to work through your merged money plan. First things first: uncover your beliefs and stories about money. And then release those as stories of the past. Once you know your money story, you are going to create a spending plan that honors both wishes—yours and your partner's—and takes care of your current needs and bigger wants. Ruth says in her book:

---

11 1. Ruth L. Hayden, *For Richer, Not Poorer: The Money Book for Couples* (Deerfield Beach, FL: Health Communications, 1999).

FINISH FINANCIALLY **FREE**

"Deciding to Put Forth the Effort to Create a Change in Your Money Life is the Only Way You Can Create Real, Lasting Change"

The most challenging part of all of this will be compromising. Answering questions like, "How do you get yours while I get mine?" and "How are we going to make our budget work?" is the language that Ruth refers to as creative compromise. It's a skill that you will learn and develop over time. This is all built on the foundation of trust.

You and your partner will meet weekly to discuss the goals and how the prior week went with the goals of the budget. She goes into great detail on how using the envelope system or something similar to it can provide a visual of what comes up short and where there might be a little extra wiggle room. For instance, if you had budgeted $200 a week for groceries and don't seem to have enough food to live off of by the end of the week, perhaps you are going to have to move some funds from some other envelope (like entertainment?) or change how and where you grocery shop. In your weekly check-in, you can review not only the numbers and what needs to be changed around in order to make it work, but also check in emotionally. This process of following a budgeted plan and making cuts and tracking dollars may trigger some unforeseen and uncomfortable feelings that need to be discussed before it becomes an explosive fight. Just remember you have done hard things before, and you deserve to have your money working for your family goals. It feels so great to be in sync with the bigger goals and celebrate successes when the money is working for you.

Remember it is important that each of you gets their needs (and possibly desires and wants) met. I have seen where one person in the relationship is a spender and just has to have every little desire fulfilled. If that is you, consider that your wanting mind is really going to affect not only your immediate goals of making your monthly money work for you but also hinder your larger goals. And honestly, it's not fair. You can't be the one getting and getting and getting while your partner forfeits getting some desires met (and even if they don't "want" for anything, consider they don't "want" because there isn't much money to go towards their wants after feeding yours or that the savings goal is much more important to them than a want).

Keep in mind that one of you may feel inferior when it comes to money. Because it's not a comfortable thing to deal with, there may be a lack of confidence based on prior results from money mismanagement; or if one of you earns less than the other, they may feel inferior to you and may not feel like they have a say in the money goals. Be aware of these as possibilities of emotions. Just because it's not said doesn't mean those feelings don't exist. Having that scheduled weekly meeting where it's a safe place built around a commitment to figure out a plan to make your household money go as far as possible towards hitting your goals and desires will really help the plan start to take form.

Be committed to each other and your written goals. I cannot stress enough that if you both aren't in this together, the plans will not turn into actions that result in hitting your target. It's possible that together you slip up or maybe just one of you will slip but be fully committed to the plan you create and make adjustments as you see fit. But if it's just one of you, this will not work and you may find yourself having the same fight time after time. Most couples don't fight about everything—most fight about the same few issues they can't seem to have a breakthrough in. I believe you can have a breakthrough but you both have to be on board 100 percent!

The plan from *For Richer, Not Poorer* looks like this (you will have your own):

STEP 1: Write down what you want to have, what you want to do, who you want to be, and what you want to see. All of your dreams. Some will be shared, some of them will be your own goals.

STEP 2: Create a time frame for these dreams and hopes. You will create a six-month goal, two years from now, five years from now, ten years from now, and then an age that you consider to be "old age." How many years from now will that be? Write that down.

STEP 3: Fit your hopes and dreams from Step 1 into the time frame you created in Step 2. What will it take to make those time frames happen?

STEP 4: Work together to set goals. She says, "All couples have hopes, dreams, assumptions, and expectations that are unspoken to each other. It is these unspoken assumptions that create problems."

STEP 5: For each time frame, discuss and then write down a couple of strategies to make all three sets of goals work: yours, mine, and ours.

This part should be a lot of fun! I love dreaming and scheming. It's fun to come up with wild or even practical ways to make these dreams a reality. Compromise is not giving something up—it's finding a happy middle ground. This is where you will ask questions like:

- » Where do you need to compromise your individual goals?
- » How do you need to think differently about your lives?
- » How will you make your goals, your partner's goals, and your goals as a couple work within each time frame?

This next statement the author shares hit me in the heart: *This incongruity between what they thought they would do with their lives and what they actually did creates great sadness for many people. Your values need to be included in your budget planning so you can be sure they're not just words but the foundation of your life.*

Do make sure your goals include things that are important to you, such as tithing regularly, giving to your favorite nonprofit, or supporting a cause you are passionate about.

There are big consequences for not setting written goals and having a plan to get to those goals. You may find that if you don't have an assignment for every dollar received, it will have plans of its own. You need to agree that future earnings will be added to the discussion—job promotions, business success, bonuses and raises, inheritance, or insurance payout—life can throw some crazy things your way, for the good. Just make sure to agree by taking a little time to discuss a plan for the money rather than just handling it when it comes along. Having an agreement now for the future (unexpected but very appreciated) money will help you make it work the hardest for you. I have seen so many people not have a plan and never discuss it, and a large amount of cash is blown away like a dandelion in the wind. Poof. Don't let that be you. Pinky promise today that you will create a plan and even bring in others such as a financial advisor, trusted mentor, or a caring and wise relative (such as a parent or grandparent if you believe they are wise with their money but do use caution when bringing in family!) to get guidance on best practices with a large sum of money.

So, take a deep breath. How are you feeling? Does this sound like something you can tackle together? Everything is easier to tackle with someone on your team. I hope this is a great start to get in conversation and start brainstorming your big life goals so you can take action and support each other's goals. Just thinking about that vision of talking it through and brainstorming ideas and ways to make an awesome future happen makes me smile; because unfortunately, I work with a lot of people going through a divorce. I can't help but wonder if they would have had a chance at winning at life-long partnership if they had had a few tools to open the conversation and have the uncomfortable but necessary talk to take action together and master their money.

CHAPTER 5

MONEY PERSONALITIES

In an earlier chapter, we discussed how our core personalities are shaped in our formative years and how they are more difficult to change than our beliefs. There are parts of our personality that can show up differently depending on circumstances. For example, certain traits of my personality show up when I am spending time with my closest friends or family versus people I have just met or how I "show up" at work. So, let's segment that portion of our personality as it relates to money.

We have money personalities that express our beliefs and relationship with money. There are many different types of money personalities, and I have read many books and have taken several courses about the various money personality types. Just like our core personalities, money personalities are partly genetic but are strongly affected by our environment, what our family and experiences "taught" us growing up, and how something (in this case, money) made you feel. Remember, some people repel it, and some people chase it. Some people spend it (even when they don't have it or they spend it as soon as they do have it), and some people hold on tight to every last cent.

Below is an overview of what I have put together as money personality descriptions. I have combined several personality types into one of six categories. Once we review the definition of each category (and there is a good likelihood you are not only one, although one may be more dominant than the other money personality you have), I will share some alternative behaviors to bring balance to those principles that are running your decisions and your life. You may find that you connect with one or two of the statements but not all definitions of each category, and that is normal. You likely won't relate to every example in the category that you find to be your dominant money personality.

Spenders, Shoppers, Pleasure Seekers, Strivers

Use it or lose it. Impulsive. Shopping = therapy! Thrill from the shopping or spending. Attracted to shiny and new, brand names, and the newest gadgets. Not searching for a bargain but the "buy." If it feels good, it must be right. Showing others: I have what it takes. Not worried about debt. Experiences great enjoyment when shopping or spending. Emotionally satisfied when spending/buying something new. Money is a status symbol. Feels important or increases self-esteem when spending money.

MONEY PERSONALITIES

Savers, Guardians, Hoarders, Security Seekers, Squirrels, Amassers

Frugal. Not concerned about latest trends. Doesn't need shiny and new. Careful, cautious, or alert with money. May never feel like they "have enough." Doesn't enjoy what they already have. Won't pay interest. Investigates and shops endlessly for the cheapest deal. Hates spending money. Conservative. No risk-taking. Will give up quality to save money. Money = self-worth or power. Wants to watch the bank balance grow. It feels safe to have money in the bank. Very protective of bank balance and can be called stingy. Think Scrooge.

Avoiders, Ostriches, Optimistic, Withdrawn, Flyers, Innocent

Money is complicated. What about it? Things will take care of itself. I will worry about it next year. I'm not smart enough to figure out money. I don't deserve money. Powerless. Life will work it out for the best. I am not competent enough to figure this out. I am no good with money. I can get easily overwhelmed when having to make money decisions. Not interested in financial planning, following a budget, or giving money much thought.

Risk Takers, High Rollers, Empire Builders

Nothing ventured, nothing gained. Excited by possibility. Bets against the odds. Optimistic with the potential for money growth. Impatient. Impulsive but decisive. Can make more and more and more. Gambler. Takes chances. For the thrill of it. Seeking big payoffs. Many investors and entrepreneurially-minded people are risk-takers. Focused on gain, not potential loss.

FINISH FINANCIALLY FREE

Debtors, Investors, Debt Desperados
Spends no time thinking about money. Doesn't keep tabs on spending. No budget and no idea where the money goes. Typically maxed on credit card balances and has many loans. Not investing in financial future, just feeding credit card payments. Everything owned is bought on credit. Making payments on everything from cell phone to furniture.

Give-Away-ers, Money Monks, Caretakers
Gives away money because may view money as the root of all evil. Money is bad. Money can ruin things. Doesn't love money. Money is only used to take care of others. I am not meant to keep/have money. If I don't pay their bill, who will take care of them? Giving it away expresses compassion and love.

A lot of the time, you will find yourself in a dominant money personality, and you will likely see many secondary personality attributes in you. Reflect back on your money story that you had discovered earlier in this book. You had uncovered your core beliefs about money. Do you now see how your beliefs shaped your money personality?

Has your money personality changed over time? Was there a significant event or experience that you went through that has shaped your beliefs and money personality? Do you find that many of the characteristics you have mimic someone in your family (often a parent or main caretaker)?

How do you feel about what you have learned about your money personality? Just like with your core personality, it's not easily changed. But it doesn't have to be anything different than what it is. Different money personality types create different behaviors; some work for you and result in positive actions

MONEY PERSONALITIES

while some work against you and keep you stuck in patterns that aren't serving you well. By identifying your money personality type, you will be better equipped to recognize your negative default behaviors and actions, and then balance those with these counterbalancing suggestions.

Let's begin by uncovering just a little more about your thoughts. Are there thoughts you have that you will feel safe, satisfied, happy, or fulfilled if only you had this one [thing, experience, amount of money in the bank, job title, relationship, education, address, etc.]? Each person has something unique to them that drives them. For me, I feel safe when I have at least six months of living expenses in the emergency fund and the credit card balance paid in full. For someone else, it might be driving a certain car or owning a home in a prestigious part of town. Really dig deep and uncover what it is that would truly make you feel safe, satisfied, happy, and fulfilled. Knowing this will also help you put together your short- and long-term goals so that you will experience those feelings you are longing for.

I will feel safe/satisfied when_____

_____

If only I could have_____ ,
then I would be happy.
What I want more than anything is _____

_____

My dominant money personality type is:_____

_____

Now that you have identified your dominant and then second (and maybe even a third!) money personality type, it's important to focus on replacing the behaviors that have kept you stuck and get in the way of accomplishing your goals. There's a good likelihood that your partner is the opposite of your personality, so make sure you discuss the positives, negatives, and suggestions together to better understand each other. Ready? Let's do this!

Spenders, Shoppers, Pleasure Seekers, Strivers

If this is your personality, you are often the one buying "the first round," have a blast shopping, drive a nice car, and are fashionable with name brands. You are buying on credit to have now rather than saving for later. You aren't shopping for a bargain. You simply get what you want and don't want to wait. You are likely spending all the money you earn and have several (more likely many) credit cards that have constant balances on them and personal loans. You finance your brand-new phone, new furniture, new car, your awesome vacation, and that high-end purse or expensive shoes. No savings to speak of. Your friends enjoy being around you because of your generosity and the pleasure new things brings to you, but they might feel uncomfortable with the spending if they are a savers type of personality.

POSITIVE TRAITS: Generous, enjoys what money can buy, carefree (this one is also a negative!).

NEGATIVE TRAITS: Impulsive, carefree, stretched on credit with maxed or almost maxed balances, often living on credit cards to have the shiny new thing, often has no savings.

COUNTERBALANCING SUGGESTIONS: Set up automatic withdrawals from each paycheck for a forced savings account, follow a simple budget just to see and know where the money is going, consider implementing a wait rule (say, forty-eight hours) before making a large purchase, make a game out of saving a certain percentage of your income before you can go shopping and then enjoy it! Name your savings account: college fund, home purchase, dream vacation, etc., and consider budgeting an allowance. You must stay inside of that spending allowance each week; it forces you to prioritize your shopping/spending. Consider a side hustle for additional spending money since the thought of cutting expenses sounds less likely than making more money. Find a replacement for your shopping therapy: reading, running, or a hobby/distractor that doesn't cost you a lot of mullah!

Savers, Guardians, Hoarders, Security Seekers, Squirrels, Amassers

If this is your personality, then watching your bank balance grow is your aim in life! It helps you feel secure. You likely keep your AC at a nearly uncomfortable temperature to not waste money on electricity, yell at the fam about keeping the refrigerator door open too long, and live very frugally. You follow a budget to the dime and likely have nothing allocated for pleasantries or money just to have for buying something on a whim. Although you don't see yourself as a cheapskate, you may forfeit fun experiences, dinners out, or vacations because you don't want to spend the money on things that aren't important to you (your bank balance is what's most important!). But your relationships may suffer if taken to an extreme. Spending is uncomfortable. You will be the one able to retire at a decent age and have funds in a retirement, although you will likely work later in your years than you have to because to you, your savings may never be quite . . . enough.

POSITIVE TRAITS: Takes pride in saving and a big bank balance. Unlikely to fall into financial ruin, conservative and careful/

cautious with money, safe or low-risk investments, retirement accounts are likely fully getting funded each year.

NEGATIVE TRAITS: Worry, anxiety, playing it safe, can't enjoy what they have, it's never enough, fearful, overly obsessed with bank balances or collecting, keeping, and/or investing money.

COUNTERBALANCING SUGGESTIONS: Everything in moderation! Don't let life pass you by to save a few pennies or dollars. Consider spreading a little of your savings into a type of investment that can yield you a little more than your "safe" savings or money market accounts. If you earn a little more on your investments, you can give yourself permission to use those extra monies for your family or friends to enjoy doing things with you that require you to part from your money. Consider it as upgrading your current quality of life rather than parting from money.

Avoiders, Ostriches, Optimistic, Withdrawn, Flyers, Innocent

If this is you, listen up! Ignoring doesn't make the reality go away. Your personality leads you and others to believe you just "aren't a money person" or it's too hard to figure out. So, you just disregard learning or planning financially. Perhaps your parents never taught you about money. It feels elusive and challenging, and you just have no desire to take on the chore of learning this money thing. You may believe money is bad or you don't deserve to have it. Status quo is good enough. Money is likely the last thing on your mind. You believe, it will work out, somehow . . .

POSITIVE TRAITS: Not stressed about finances, doesn't fight or debate about money.

NEGATIVE TRAITS: Bills are often ignored or paid late, doesn't know bank balance, no budget, gets anxious about big money decisions, feels inadequate or incompetent when it comes to money decisions, has no idea how much is owed, how much has been saved, or how much has been spent. Possible low credit scores and damaged credit profile. Others in your life may feel frustrated by your attitude of ignoring money decisions or not caring about the outcome.

COUNTERBALANCING SUGGESTIONS: Find a Money Mentor: friend or financial advisor, use a simple budget, consider using the Mint app for simple online budgeting where you don't have to deal with anything other than inputting initial info. Put "set-it-and-forget-it" style retirement accounts at work, set up automatic drafts from each paycheck into an online savings account. Believe that you deserve money and once you believe this, seek out some basic knowledge and understanding. Nothing complicated to understand like annuities or day trading, you just need to start with paying bills on time and building a savings account.

Risk Takers, High Rollers, Empire Builders

If this is your personality, you get a thrill out of the possibility of what your money can do, not money itself. You could have all the money in the world and still chase after the next big thing for the fun of the chase. You believe 'no risk, no reward' and see "safe" investments as a way to keep your money stagnate. There's no fun in safe! Not worried about the details. You trust your gut and your advisors, and you are quick to make decisions. You can be viewed as adventurous and enjoy taking chances. You want to be at the ground level of something that has the opportunity to be something huge, even if you

FINISH FINANCIALLY FREE

risk losing what you put into it. You seek big payoffs, and you are optimistic once you get involved in an investment of your money. Focused on gain and not the potential of loss.

POSITIVE TRAITS: Optimistic, intuitive, adventurous, fearless, entrepreneur mindset, determined.

NEGATIVE TRAITS: Vulnerable, impatient, gambler, may think you are invincible, trusts "luck" and can be conned because you tend to trust people that have a great sales pitch.

COUNTERBALANCING SUGGESTIONS: Diversify your portfolio, add in a little stability with some long-term growth focus, allow a few risk-adverse investment strategies, just because! Ensure that the risk you are going to take isn't going to use every penny you have. Much like when I go to Vegas, I bring play money and that is all I have to gamble with to allow money for food, drinks, and shows while we are there. If you increase your money through gambling, go big if you want to on your earnings, but don't bet your dinner money just to fill the thrill. I don't want to see you desolate because you went all-in on a deal that went south.

Debtors: Investors, Debt Desperados

If you have more credit cards in your wallet than dollars, you are likely a debtor. Everything you buy is on credit, either offered by a store or racked up on your bank-issued credit cards like a Discover Card or Citicard. You have never had a car paid off before, you leverage financing on everything you own. You likely have a negative net worth because what you owe is greater than what you own. You don't spend much time thinking about money or keeping tabs on where you spend it or even how much you spend. You spend more than you bring in and do not contribute to 401(k) or retirement plans. Simply put, you aren't investing in your financial future. If you lean more toward the investor personality, you are forward-thinking and leveraging/financing your current lifestyle in pursuit of your investment goals, likely in stocks or real estate. Putting yourself in debt today, seeking passive income one day, and in constant thought about the end goal of making your money work for you rather than working for money.

POSITIVE TRAITS: Accumulating 'stuff' to enjoy and the investor is typically purchasing money-making instruments such as rental properties.

NEGATIVE TRAITS: Often buried in debt, slave to creditors, earning income just to pay debts.

COUNTERBALANCING SUGGESTIONS: Set up automatic savings deposits out of your paychecks before you even see your income, write out long-term savings goals, balance "right now" with the future. Consider a side hustle to earn more money to pay down the balances you carry and follow a simple budget to help you pay more attention to what is going on with your credit cards. Make a promise to pay down what you have before you buy something on credit.

Give-Away-ers: Money Monks, Caretakers

If any of these are your personality type, you get rid of money as soon as it comes to you. You have a deeply ingrained belief that money is bad or the root of all evil. Perhaps someone in your distant past used it against you or as a weapon. You might simply believe money is meant for others and not you and have a tendency to just give it away rather than creating a plan for your money and saving it for your retirement, education, or other goals. A lot of this behavior style is based on not feeling worthy to have money. The lie is: It's meant for others to have, not you. I also see plenty of people "taking care of others" as a co-dependent way of being in a relationship by taking care of others' financial needs or burdens and mistakes, constantly bailing them out at the cost of your own savings.

POSITIVE TRAITS: Helpful and caring to those you care about, generous giver to those in need, often supportive of charities and organizations that do "good" in the world.

NEGATIVE TRAITS: No savings for the future, your actions reinforce that money is not meant for you, you may be at risk of being taken advantage of by others and enabling them to continue to count on you and never be able to retire because once you stop working, where will the money come from to survive?

COUNTERBALANCING SUGGESTIONS: Create a forced savings account that 20 percent of your net income flows into. This will at least fund an emergency savings for when you need something taken care of and also start a savings for **you**. You can't give away what's not in your operating (checking) account so keep this money separate and unavailable to others that tend to rely on you to bail them out or support them. This is for you, and you *are* worthy of having savings for your needs. See if you can help empower those who constantly suck your money away and consider that your behavior in giving them money is not serving them well. Find a new way to support them—perhaps by encouragement or introducing them to resources that can better serve them. There are financial counselors and financial advisors that can do the work for you and help make money work for you and still allow your funds to be given away to others if this is truly important to you, but in moderation—take care of yourself first. Liken this thought to you placing your own oxygen mask on before helping those with you, as in an emergency on a flight. I want you to be in a good financial spot with savings first before you give away the farm.

Now that you have clarity on your money personality, you are clear on the behavior styles that accommodate that personality and have suggestions on how to counterbalance the negative traits, so let's build on this knowledge and uncover how psychology plays a huge part in our money.

CHAPTER 6

PSYCHOLOGY IN MONEY

L et's learn a few things about how our mind works when it comes to money since our mind makes those decisions, guided by our feelings. A majority of the money we spend is driven by our emotions. The information in this chapter is from a variety of sources that have taught me some powerful things when it comes to the power our minds have over our choices and decisions. Knowing these topics will help you be aware of what is driving your decisions and what you can do about it.

Psychology is Tied to Our Money

I love paying attention to what drives people's behaviors and decisions now that I know to notice. It's all emotional. It's how something is going to make us feel. A lot of times we think something is going to make us feel good and happy and then after a purchase we feel bad about making the purchase—like buyer's remorse. Then that happiness turns into unhappiness (and often additional debt), and we still try to justify that maybe it was okay to have made this purchase. All the while feeling lousy inside about it. How do we avoid this mixed bag of feelings and how do we take control of all this? Understanding our behaviors when it comes to our finances is key. It's a matter of noticing our triggers and paying attention to the emotions before making a purchase. Then we can keep some things in check and not completely wreck and destroy our attempts at following that spending guide throughout the month. Start by accepting that most of our large purchases are emotionally driven and—this one is going to hurt—we are completely irrational beings and logic doesn't usually lead. Emotions and feelings drive our decision-making.

Now that we know the hard truth about our decision-making when it comes to what we buy and how we spend our money, let's look at how we get our money. Our "regular" income is what we tend to live off of for our regular living expenses and things we choose to purchase or experience. But what happens when we get a windfall of money? Imagine for a moment that you just bought a scratch-off and—watch out—you just won $10,000! Or you just finished a big project, and your boss bonused you $3,000. Happy dance time! What do you do with that money? There's a really good chance that you start thinking about something new you wanted to buy or wondering if your passport expired because a remote tropical island is calling your name. The truth is that how we receive money dictates how we spend our money. There are a few of you scratching your head and saying, "not me," but I see it over and over again, and the majority of people behave this way. Tax refund, gift money, lottery, etc. . . . it often gets spent very differently than our regular income. Just saying.

A few years back, I went through an online course presented by the University of Toronto called *Behavioural Economics in Action*. That is where I had learned about the topics I want to share with you in greater detail. I truly loved learning about these principles, and I see it showing up in my life all the time now. Well, it was always there, I just never gave it much attention. So please, give this some attention—it can save you a lot of money over time.

How we pay absolutely has an impact on how much we spend. Let's say you have been driving around running errands on a hot July afternoon and you need a refreshment. You swing into a corner store to grab a cold bottle of water. As you are walking towards the back of the store to get your thirst-quenching beverage, you realize you don't have any cash on you, just your credit card. There is a really good chance you pick up something else to purchase, too, as to not swipe a credit card for such a small amount. Then, the same thing happens at the grocery store. Which is why all those small but tempting treats are lined up as you stand in line for the cashier. If you walked into the grocery store with exactly one hundred dollars to buy this week's groceries, do you think your cart would look differently than if you purchased with your credit card? Likely by a decent difference, no doubt.

There is something called the transparency spectrum which states that how you pay dictates how much you spend. Most transparent on this spectrum is cash because it must physically leave your hands, and there is actual pain affiliated with the loss of that money. The next is checks, since the act of writing a check and accounting for takes a little effort. Credit cards are so easy to swipe. I know I am not alone when I get the statement and see all the charges on my credit card and notice that I "forgot" about this purchase and that purchase. And it was just a short while ago! Credit cards make it too easy and convenient that we literally forget we bought that thing or spent money at that place. The least transparent is autopay. Mostly because we are expecting it, it is typically recurring monthly and already built into our overall spending costs. Examples include housing and car payments, insurance, and cell phone bills.

SUNK AND OPPORTUNITY COSTS

There are a couple of other definitions you should know as well. If you haven't heard of sunk cost, I want to explain it now. A sunk cost means the amount you have already paid for something. It's funny what can happen in our minds when you have already paid for something versus not having paid for it. Let me give a few examples. Let's say you were planning on going to an outdoor concert. You have already purchased the ticket and the weather is quite nasty—rainy and windy—but the show will go on! There is a better likelihood you will go if you have already purchased the ticket than if you paid at the door. I had to pay for my gym membership this way in order to be all in. I knew if I paid by the month, I may decide to get lazy and end the membership and stop going. I paid for a full year—which hurt—and has me totally committed to going because I paid for it. I am getting my money's worth! Can you think of something in your life that you participate in because you have the money sunk into it? It can affect how dedicated you are to something or not, so now that you know, start paying attention if a sunk cost is the thing dictating your actions and commitment.

Opportunity cost is the cost of taking one opportunity over another opportunity. If your future wealth is invested in real estate instead of the stock market, there is an opportunity cost, likely determined by what is going on in each market at that moment. When it comes to debt, like credit cards and car loans, the money you are paying on those monthly payments keeps you from giving towards your 401(k) or savings goals where it is growing and earning you interest. Everything in life has a tradeoff. Start bringing to your awareness whether the opportunity cost of the decision is greater than, equal to, or less than the tradeoff. But it's more than financial; it applies to your time and energy as well. I tend to say yes to a lot of requests, even if it is not the highest and best use of my time. Then I get disappointed in myself for saying yes and feel like I am wasting my time on something that is not fulfilling, productive, or enjoyable. Then I make myself wrong for saying yes and it creates inner conflict for me. I am a work in progress and working on better protecting my time. Considering the opportunity costs helps me determine if it is worth my money, time, and energy.

LOSS AVERSION

You may have not heard the term, but you will be able to relate to the description. The general explanation for loss aversion is that a loss hurts more than a gain makes us happy. Let's say I called you today to tell you I had an extra ticket to see your favorite (sports team, concert, etc.). You would be stoked, right? YAY—this feels great! Good for you. Just acknowledge what that feeling is like for a moment. I bet you are pretty happy!

Now let that thought and feeling go. I didn't call you with the great news. Instead, you had printed tickets that you purchased (not electronic for the purpose of illustrating the scenario) for your favorite thing. And you got floor seats (or box seats). Those aren't cheap! But then you lost them. Your tickets were gone. The money you spent on the tickets disappeared and you were no longer able to experience your special event with amazing seats. How does that feel? LOUSY. Terrible. It's a loss. And a loss hurts more than a gain brings happiness. A loss often hurts twice as much as the happy feeling you experience with a gain. Twice the pain. Simply put, it's better not to lose something than it is to gain something. Unless it's body fat. Kidding!

   I share this with you because sometimes the fear of loss can impact our decision-making. Loss aversion can keep you from making even sound financial decisions. So just keep this in the back of your mind as you stockpile this knowledge, because there is a good chance it may come up in your thinking when you are making future financial decisions and now you can question if the fear of a loss drives your choices. You could also use this knowledge to consider a loss in the future, such as if you don't have the savings ready to jump on an incredible opportunity. Let's say one of your future goals is to own a twenty-unit apartment building twenty years from now. You would need to start saving now towards that goal for a hefty down payment required to obtain financing or the cash money to purchase it. Let's say you didn't put the money aside and twenty years from now, the most unbelievable property was presented to you at a magnificent purchase price. But you didn't have your savings ready to go. You can't purchase it. What would that loss feel like? Sometimes turning things around to benefit you in your thoughts can help drive better decisions and help you take action, without the fear leading the way.

CREATE DISRUPTERS

Think about the last time you went to the movie theater. If you are like me, you probably opted for the mega-jumbo size popcorn. Why? Because it was the only one you could halfway justify in price. I would devour the small size before the previews even started, and the medium felt like it was too small for the absurd price tag on it. So, the mega-jumbo size bucket it is. But let's pretend you go to place your order and the cashier tells you they ran out of buckets, but they will give you the equivalent size of popcorn, so you get what you paid for as far as net weight of the popcorn. You agree, she gives you five small bags, and you head to your theater. Once you get to the bottom of the first bag, which likely happens in 4.3 seconds, you start on your next bag. This is more than enough for a "single serving," but let's say you tore through the second bag. Once you get to the bottom of that bag, you have to make a decision (much like you had at the end of the first bag but may not have noticed it then), which is: do you start eating the third bag? If you had one gigantic bucket of buttery and salted popcorn, you likely wouldn't have stopped to think about how much you were devouring. Until your stomach started aching!

With these smaller bags, you have to make a decision. It forces you to stop and think. And then you have to consider a few things. In this example, do I really want more popcorn? Am I still hungry for it, craving it? Did I have enough? Am I satisfied or could I be satisfied? Is this next bag going to make me feel lousy or will I enjoy it? This disrupter has actually created a buffer from overdoing it, or at least has created an opportunity for you to stop and think. It might make you pause, see how you feel, and decide if you even want any more popcorn at that moment.

FINISH FINANCIALLY FREE

See how many ways you can create disrupters in your life that cause you to pause and require your brain to think for a moment instead of just going through the motions? If you tend to snack at nine o'clock and want to scale it back instead of grabbing the entire Oreos package, grab five out of the package and put the remainder up high in the closet that would require you to get up from your comfy couch to go get more. It makes you stop to think—but it might also make you more fully appreciate the five yummy treats you do have, which might be just enough to curb your sweet tooth.

Perhaps when it comes to spending, you can stop to ask yourself if this is a need or a want, and if it is a want that is larger than one hundred dollars, consider putting a twenty-four-hour disrupter on it to think about it, sleep on it. Maybe you find the next day that you don't want it after all. Putting aside cash for the items you have budgeted for creates a disrupter. Think about this. Let's say you have designated one hundred dollars a week for groceries. If you walked into the grocery store with a one hundred dollar bill, you have created a disrupter by having to calculate the costs of each item you put in your cart to not exceed the cash in your pocket. But if you had a credit card, you may not have thought twice.

Even our smart watches create disrupters, like letting you know when you have been stationary or sitting for too long. This helps break up time and get you into action. Start looking for other items in your life where you can create a disrupter (like finding that you spend hours on social media, but you really only want to cap it at one hour a day). You could create an alarm that after fifteen minutes, you jump off and cap it at checking in only four times a day. That alarm sets those boundaries, and this disrupter can keep you focused on your goal of not getting pulled into sucking hours of your day away on your apps. But don't be that person that ignores the alarm! Stick to your word with integrity. If you told yourself that you would honor that alarm, honor it. If you can't keep your word to yourself, how are you going to keep your word to other people? Set those boundaries, create those disrupters, and stick to them!

Now that you better understand how much psychology plays in our money-making decisions, we can use this new awareness to help propel our decision-making when it comes to how we handle our money. Talk about gaining control! It starts with our understanding and shows up in our actions.

Let's discover why many people feel caught in a never-ending hamster wheel of being unable to get ahead, to save, or to pay down debt. Then we can start learning about how to implement change.

CHAPTER 7

THE BROKE TRAP

I remember being a young kid and earning my allowance. I realize not everyone had an allowance, but my mom paid us about fifty cents a week! I know, wow, quit bragging, right?! Eventually, as we got a little older and had the ability to take on more chores, I think we got up to two dollars a week! Either way, I remember earning this money through my chore list, and the question from the adults was always, "How are you going to spend it?" Fast forward to the current day, this makes me ponder a bit on what was being ingrained in my young mind with that question. I was expected to spend what I earned. I realized it was not intentional, but those words prompted me to think about how and where I was going to spend my money. I wish I were taught to look at my earnings differently. What if the expectation from the start was that I would save 20 percent, give 10 percent towards helping someone else out, such as at church or for a fundraiser, and that I could do whatever I please with the remaining 70 percent? If that lesson were instilled from the very start, I know my money decisions would have been different all along. But many years before my first job, my brain was trained to spend what I earned. I bet I am not alone in learning that behavior.

Post-education, when we go out on our own, it seems to be just a matter of survival for many of us. We are often paid minimum wage or a low income compared to those who have many years of experience above ours. So, it absolutely makes sense how we don't have money in savings. But even as we earn more, we tend to spend more instead of creating margin or a little padding to create a savings account. And perhaps you've had the experience of creating a savings account only for it to be stripped away because of some accident or emergency that comes along. If there's anything we can plan for, it is to be ready to ignite Plan B. Our best-laid plans can often get derailed by life's little mishaps. The bigger picture here is there will always be something that comes along, so expect the unexpected when it comes to expenses.

There is a huge population of people that cannot cover a $400 emergency without putting it on a charge card or having to borrow from someone. That was me. I was included in that statistic for many years. With no savings when an emergency happens—and it will *always* happen—what do you do? With no savings, we often end up putting it on a credit card. And because this thing was unplanned, there's a good chance that we cannot pay off the balance in full. That balance accumulates interest often at the pace of the minimum payment, and maybe we use the card a little more. No wonder the average American carries a credit card balance of over

$9,300! Many people are spending money they don't have on those credit cards for non-necessities (just fulfilling their wants), with no plan or ability to repay it right away, so it accumulates interest.

> **There is a huge population of people that cannot cover a $400 emergency without putting it on a charge card or having to borrow from someone.**

Now we have an "over-utilization" of credit card balances which hurts our credit scores. Then your credit score is lowered, which now charges you higher interest rates on things you have to borrow for. Those with credit scores in the 500s or low 600s could be facing a car loan with rates in the teens or even the twenties. That is TERRIBLE and has most of your payments going towards interest, meaning you will feel like you may never pay that car off because so little of your payment is actually paying down the amount you have borrowed. Plus, your monthly payment is obnoxious with a high-interest rate, which cuts into money that should be for other things in your life. Being caught in this trap can dig you deeper because what happens when you need to make car repairs? It's easy to give up on that payment that doesn't seem to make a dent in the overall balance anyway and just hand over the keys, defeated, and ending up with a repossession or rolling negative equity into your next car, taking on even greater debt.

If everything costs you more, then no wonder there is nothing "left" to save. And then with no savings, the cycle continues with having to borrow for nearly everything.

FINISH FINANCIALLY FREE

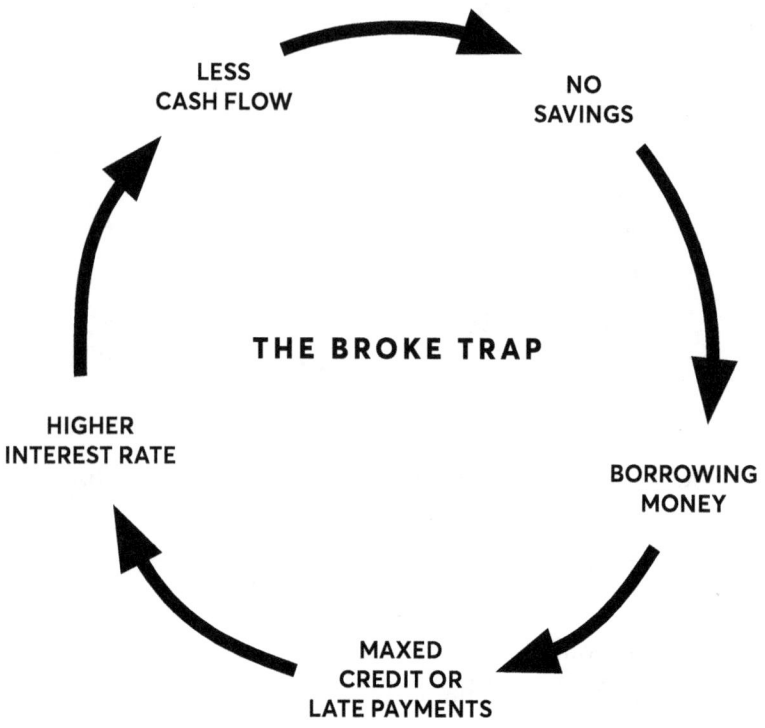

If I had learned from the very start to save before I spend, my habits and my finances would have been very different. I am grateful for the lesson; I just wish I could have stopped learning lessons the hard way! Perhaps that is the only way I learn—to feel it in the deepest part of my core where it hurts so badly, I say to the universe, "Okay! I got it! Lesson learned, stop beating me up!"

Even the smallest actions can create big results if you stick with them. And that may be the hardest part of all this that we are talking about in this book—actually sticking to a plan. Our current world has created the need for everything to be immediate. We have an appetite for a quick fix, a magic pill, or maybe even a magic eraser. But great things usually take some time to be fully realized. Think of an acorn. It can't become a mighty oak tree in just a few short years. If you need some more examples of things that can only be fully realized when due after waiting for its time, let's think of wine. Mostly because I love wine! I know when I am drinking a delicious glass of wine, it took time in the barrels and has also been bottled for what might be many years. Some things we can't rush. And we are going to be okay with that because I am going to show you and teach you many things that, over time, can make you a multimillionaire. But let's begin with a little nugget.

Tiny Wins, Compounded Over Time, Create Massive Results

You have probably heard of the term compounding. It means adding on top of what is there. It can help or hurt, depending on its context. If you work out regularly, you can see muscle tone develop, building on top of what is there. If you eat ice cream every night, eventually you may find yourself a few pounds or sizes larger than desired. It adds on top of what is there. It compounds. When it comes to interest, you make your credit card payment towards the balance and interest accrued (added on). If you carry that balance to the next month (not paying it off in full), it has compounded. In the opposite direction, when you have investments, or even just savings that accrue interest, you earn interest on the balance plus interest. And it compounds (accumulates) over time. This is where the real power is—the accumulation. So, let's get started.

FINISH FINANCIALLY FREE

Just for now, we are going to start with 5 percent of your paycheck. My bank allows me to set up many savings accounts and I could do it online quite easily. Read the fine print (I know that part sucks) and just make sure you understand what kind of balance needs to be kept in order to avoid any monthly service fees. I have found that many banks require a $500 balance or greater in order to keep the savings account free. Once you have your savings account set up, you can log into your payroll company and add this second account. Most payroll companies will allow you to choose how your paycheck gets distributed, either by specifying a specific dollar amount or a percentage of the take-home pay.

By setting it up through your payroll company, you don't even see it. You will learn to live off what is deposited into your checking account. Your goal will be to then work your way to 10 percent of your take-home pay going into your savings. And then eventually, to 20 percent. If you are just starting off with earning your paycheck for the first time, jump right into allocating 20 percent to your savings account. You won't know how to live off 100 percent of your take-home pay then! You will learn to live off 80 percent of your take-home pay from the start. Anytime you get a raise or a bonus, consider moving it into your savings account. It's your money to do with what you want. But if you are anything like me, if it stays in your checking account, it tends to get spent.

I know many people that look at their bank balance and how much time is left until their next payday. If you've deducted what your costs are going to be that will be withdrawn and paid for, and you have a little extra left in your checking account, that tends to be your fun money to spend on anything you want. The problem with that method is that you may *never* get ahead, you will never have your money actually working for you, you will only always be working for your money. And since there wasn't a plan for those "extra" few dollars, you would likely spend it on something that doesn't really bring you joy (if you can even remember what you spent it on). So, let's get out of that habit so we're not stuck in it like a trap.

Could you imagine what life would have looked like if you had started saving 10 percent at age fifteen or whenever you got your first paycheck and kept that habit going? For me, I wouldn't have had to borrow tens of thousands of dollars for college, which took me way too long to pay off. I wouldn't have had car payments, because I could have paid cash and then used what would have been a car payment to build up that cash stash again.

Let's start today. No savings = a trap. It's a vicious cycle that is very difficult to get out of. It took me working three jobs to get some savings and pay off my many credit cards, student loans, and eventually my car. I would have preferred the other way of learning the lesson—the lesson where someone said, "Hey, from the very start, put 20 percent of what you earn over in this account and let it grow towards your life's biggest goals." So, hear my voice now and change your own cycle! Maybe this small adjustment will give you hope and encouragement to boldly and colorfully see your dreams begin to take shape in your reality.

Now that we know what keeps us broke, let's learn some financial basics so we can start laying the foundation to finish financially free.

CHAPTER 8

FINANCIAL LITERACY— THE BASICS

I have heard every excuse and reason as to why someone isn't where they want to be or desire to be or could be "If only"... fill in the blank. "If only I was taught about money," "If only I had better examples," "If only I had more money to work with," "If only I hadn't made all of those mistakes in the past." No more excuses and reasons. Let's learn it already. And it doesn't have to be complicated. The basics are just the basics.

Many people never try to learn about money because of beliefs that they don't deserve to have it, might not ever have it, are still living through prior experiences mixed with poor judgment or mistakes, or getting buried in debt for a variety of reasons.

Some of the most common mistakes include:

» Not clearly defining how much money is needed to live the lifestyle they desire

FINISH FINANCIALLY FREE

» Lacking a clear financial plan
» Not having trusted mentors or advisors and taking advice from the wrong people (salespeople, family, friends)
» Poor financial choices due to lack of financial knowledge or emotions (greed and fear motivate most choices)
» A few problems that snowballed into larger problems
» Unrealistic investment return expectations
» Poor financial habits developed at a young age

When we start off with no plan, no experience, and thus no confidence, we can make decisions that turn out to be mistakes that can compound. Poor financial habits do not fix themselves and usually show up as excessive credit card debt, personal and student loans, and no money in the bank.

Let's forgive ourselves if that was your experience and focus on what you need to know how to move forward. Financial literacy is literally understanding what to do with what you have. It's knowing your numbers and knowing what the numbers mean (not like accounting, which makes my stomach uneasy), but just having a plan and understanding that it will work for you when you follow it. That is what this whole book is about, getting past our past and creating our future. Financial literacy is understanding financial elements, knowledge of what affects our money behaviors, and how our decisions impact our lives. The core concepts of personal finance are an understanding of credit, budgeting, and saving/investing.

FINANCIAL LITERACY—THE BASICS

Below is a visual of the main areas of money management:

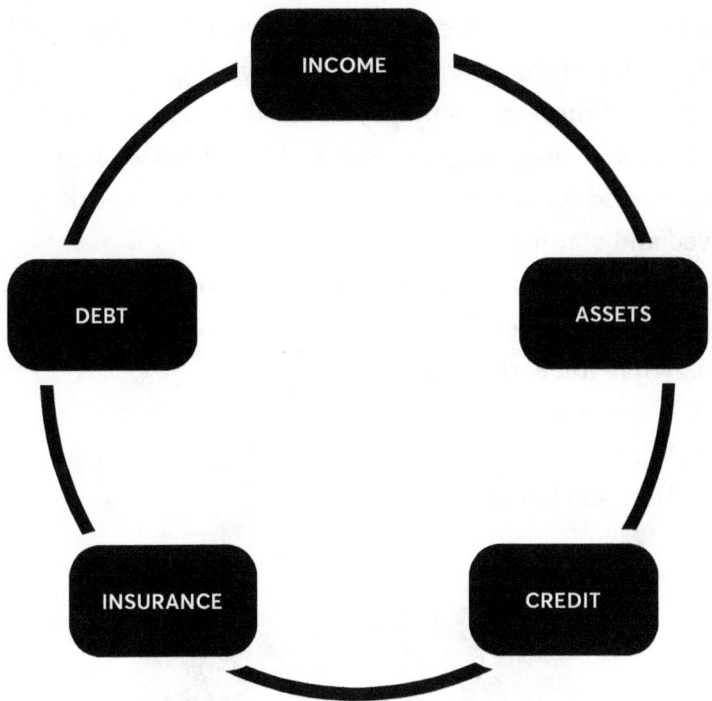

Financial literacy is as simple as knowing how much you can afford to spend based on your earnings, taking your savings into consideration, and giving and investing goals. It's knowing how much you can afford to borrow for things like your house (25 percent of your take-home pay) and your car (10 percent of your take-home pay), and then protecting all that you have worked for (with insurance).

This book serves to teach you the fundamentals of finance and ultimately help you create your plan to achieve all your goals. What do you think the number one reason is that most people can't get to this point of learning basics and creating a plan? I believe it's because they are buried in debt and can't see past the growing balances and hefty monthly payments. I have seen thousands of credit reports over the years in my line of work and it is so difficult to see hundreds if not thousands of dollars in monthly payments going toward paying back debt. Because of those monthly payments, there isn't anything left to go towards dreams, goals, and the kind of fun we are seeking such as paid-for vacations and experiences (because they were saved and planned for).

In this book, we will be focusing on four main factors of money management:

1. What you earn
2. What you spend
3. What you save
4. How you invest

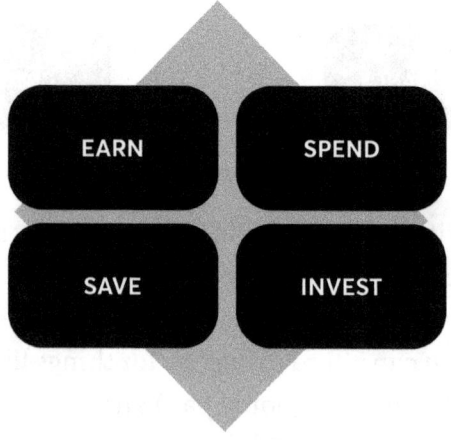

> Once we can grasp what our beliefs about money are and how they have kept us stuck, we can get into action to eliminate this needless stressor called debt.

FINANCIAL LITERACY—THE BASICS

Financial freedom starts with eliminating bad debt. There is an entire chapter dedicated to explaining debts and understanding the cost of interest as well as how to pay debt off rapidly. Once we free up the hundreds of dollars a month that was going toward servicing debt payments (credit card balances and loans), then you can start allocating that monthly amount towards goals for your dream wedding, your next car paid in cash, buying your first or next home, maxing out your retirement and investment accounts, and having more fun experiences in your life!

My life shifted so drastically when I was no longer a slave to thousands owed in credit card debt, personal loans, student loans, and a hefty car payment. I want that for you, too. Once we can grasp what our beliefs about money are and how they have kept us stuck, we can get into action to eliminate this needless stressor called debt.

A key element is managing your income. Honestly, I think there are a lot of people out there that aren't getting paid their value. They stay in their job out of comfort or complacency (or even laziness) and miss out on earning a much larger income by bringing their skillset and experience to another company. And there are many people who earn great incomes but spend every dime of it. There is nothing allocated to saving and growing the money. The problem is, when you stop working you stop earning (if you work for someone). Managing where your money is being allocated is the difference between where you are today (possibly broke or close to it) and one day becoming wealthy. The next chapter is dedicated to knowing your numbers: where you are now and where you aim to be. You can't manage what you don't measure, so seeing your numbers in black and white will be a powerful exercise, although you'll likely not like your current results. The good news is that you don't have to stay there. This is your opportunity to see what needs to be managed and altered to get you to your dream goals.

If you are not making enough, work on upgrading your value. What skills can you develop, what training you can get, what experience can you master that can afford a higher income because you bring more value? The jobs I worked at the beginning of my working years were entry-level and paid accordingly. Once I got work experience, training, education, and specialized skills, I was able to start making more money. I don't want to write too much about your employment choices other than you get paid more for your specialized expertise. Develop yourself in such a way that you can make more because of what you deliver to the marketplace.

When it comes to spending, you have 100 percent control over that. Sure, it's expensive to live. But there are ways to keep our spending in check. I had shared earlier about how much of our spending is emotionally driven in seeking a level of status in the eyes of others. Be careful not to use credit cards and loans as an extension of your income. They aren't! Focus on debt elimination. When it comes to how and what we spend, you will learn in the next chapter how to follow a plan and incorporate forced savings into that plan. If you spend everything you make (or more), you are going to feel like you are on a hamster wheel for the rest of your life. That sounds exhausting. Saving and storing some of what you make—not spending it all—will be key to accomplishing your goals and obtaining your dreams.

You are going to learn how your savings compound and earn money on your money and how to set up automatic systems to fund those dreams. Income is only one way that you bring in money, but you can also earn interest on your savings and investments, receive dividends from stocks, and create passive income such as investing in real estate or having a business that earns money even when you aren't working in the business (being a business owner does not mean having to be a business operator). But it will take savings to be able to buy those investments, stocks, real estate, and/or businesses.

You will soon have all the pieces lined up to be working for you, with a plan for when you will accomplish each savings goal. An important tip to know and start off with is to protect your income and assets. This is by having life insurance. I know what you are thinking—but just consider this for a moment. You work hard for the things you are buying in your life like your car and your home and even if you don't have a family of your own yet, you have people in your life you care about and who care about you. There are affordable life insurance policies (the younger and healthier you are, the cheaper they are) to consider. Just like you insure your car and your home, it's wise to have a life insurance policy. Most successful business owners, financial advisors, and even gurus like Dave Ramsey will tell you that life insurance is a sound fundamental basis for your financial goals.

Before we leave the topic of insurance, please make sure that you have appropriate health insurance. One of the top reasons for bankruptcy is for medical expenses that cannot be paid. There are also some supplemental insurance products that cover many things that health insurance doesn't (think AFLAC). Typically, those products can be very affordable and create another hedge of protection from possible financial costs that can cripple your goals, if not protected.

FINISH FINANCIALLY **FREE**

Now was that so painful? I didn't think so either. Now that you have a basic overview of earning, saving, spending, and investing, let's focus on how to manage what you make so you can save, spend, and invest in a way that helps you be financially free!

CHAPTER 9

RUN YOUR NUMBERS LIKE YOU'RE A BUSINESS

My guess is that you may have not launched a successful business. Most people haven't, so I am just making a presumption. I was a business owner in the past, in business with a partner. It didn't end well—so you know I have stories and beliefs I am still working through about being a business owner/partner and operator. But if and when you decide to start a business, what do you do first? Well, you search out what other people have done and what they would suggest you do, right? At least that is what I had done. You do a little research, and you create a plan. You don't just register a business name and launch a website. There's a whole lot more that goes into it.

You would create a business plan, create a budget, get financing if needed, bring in the right people or partners, create a strong brand through a strong value proposition, build out for a proper infrastructure (hardware, software, overhead, business space), and do market research: is there a need for your business, an audience that wants what you are proposing, and have you evaluated income possibilities versus the cost of doing business? Since money and finances are so personal, what if we took the emotion out of the equation as much as possible? What if we set up your finances like we would a business? Creating a plan would take the "personal" out of it. Sometimes when we are too close to something, we can't see it for what it truly is. So, if we can take a few steps back and look at it from a business perspective, perhaps then the planning and budgeting won't feel so restrictive.

There are some basic elements to a business plan that you can focus on. If you search for a basic business plan, you will find that they usually start with an executive summary, a company overview, your target audience, and market conditions to identify your competitors. You would write about your service offerings and type up some forecasts of financial needs. Last, you may talk about how you will measure your success.

Sounds a little exhausting, doesn't it? Well, the great news is you don't have to do any of that! But what you will want to put together is a snapshot of your vision of where you'd like to be one year from now, three to five years from now, and maybe even project out ten years from now. You allowed yourself to start dreaming some dreams and envision some goals to aim for more than one, three, and five years from now. By setting up your finances properly, we can take this vision and convert it into that goal.

If you are just getting started off as an adult, it could be difficult to envision where your life might be in ten years because so much will change over this next decade. But if your life is a little more established, you want to plan for your current

RUN YOUR NUMBERS LIKE YOU'RE A BUSINESS

goals and project out ten years. And the reason I brought up retirement in a prior chapter is because so many people are so busy with today, that it's nearly impossible to think about what it might be like in say, thirty years from now. Shoot, it's difficult enough to figure out how to make it to payday! And I want you to think about where your money will be when you're seventy or eighty! All I know is, if I don't create a plan to get started, I can guarantee I won't finish well, and my later years may not include all the (travel) plans I have in mind. We are simply planning for—not trying to control—the future.

If right now you are already feeling stuck, I understand. For so many years, I couldn't dream of a prosperous future because I was earning below the median income and drowning in debt between my student loans, car loan, and credit cards that had balances I couldn't seem to pay down. And you want me to write down my dream wedding (I will have to pay for)? See myself taking a real vacation? Buy my first home? It can feel daunting, out of reach, or even impossible. The purpose of this vision plan is to allow your mind to start seeing it as a possibility. You may have to give yourself permission to dream about something that at this moment in time, might just feel impossible.

Have you ever heard a story about a person who broke a record for (fill in the blank: fastest mile, highest jump, longest swim)? Once that person did it, guess what happened? All sorts of other people could then do the same thing! It's like once the brain can have an actual vision of that thing being accomplished, it says, "Well, will you look at that, it's not impossible after all, let's give it a go."

So, let's put those feelings you may be feeling aside, if even just for a moment. Allow your mind to run wild with thoughts of what would bring you great joy, fulfillment, and accomplishment if you could have or experience it. Picture yourself in that moment. Next you will have the opportunity to just start writing out a few of your goals and dreams and what you want to accomplish, just like you would if you were creating a business to present to the world. It doesn't have to be complicated, just a starting point. But the more you can envision what you desire your life to look like, the more likely it is to be accomplished.

If you can't think of any specifics, it is likely because your imagination has been a little stifled by current circumstances. Just doodle words or experiences that bring a smile to your face. Pen-to-paper tends to be the most engaging for your brain. You have permission to use a little imagination. Something we likely haven't tapped in to for a while! Use the "1-3, and 5 Year Planner" on the opposite page to do this now.

Now ask the questions: *What do I want for my life? How do I want to fill my days?* No one wants a "job;" we want the money the job provides us. So, when we are not working, how are we investing, spending, and sharing our time? If we are not intentional and purposeful, our days will fade away and any goals we have created for ourselves may never be fulfilled. I've heard it said that (paraphrased):

"The Richest Land in All the World is a Graveyard, Because That's Where Most Dreams are Buried"

RUN YOUR NUMBERS LIKE YOU'RE A BUSINESS

1-3, AND 5 YEAR PLANNER	**YEAR:**

TOP 5 GOALS FOR YEARS 1-3:

1.

2.

3.

4.

5.

WHAT NEEDS TO HAPPEN FIRST?	WHAT COULD STAND IN MY WAY?
WHO/ WHAT NEEDS TO HELP ME?	HOW WILL I CELEBRATE IT?

TOP GOALS FOR 5 YEARS FROM NOW:

1.

2.

3.

4.

5.

WHAT NEEDS TO HAPPEN BEFORE I CAN REALIZE THIS GOAL?

Isn't that heartbreaking? So many people die with their dreams inside of them. And many people lose the ability to dream big because they may have experienced so much disappointment and hurt. Many people can't even use their imagination any longer; it's like it was sent away to a penitentiary when they became adults. And if you can't tap into your imagination any longer, it's nearly impossible to envision a life that's so radically different from your current reality.

This exercise might be something you can finish in a few minutes to an hour, or you may ponder on it for days. You can always come back and add to it or refine your original thoughts. I want to encourage you right now to tap into your imagination. What does your most amazing life look like? If you think you don't want to dream that big because you don't want to feel disappointed if you fail, I have to ask: aren't you already disappointed? I know I was, living a mediocre life with a really boring routine. I'd rather feel disappointment for trying and *almost* having it all than *not* trying and wasting away.

I want to encourage you right now: write out your goals. Big ones, little ones, crazy ones. Think of those things that you buried deep inside of you, the ones you surrendered to never happening. Pull those up and write those down. As long as they are your dreams, then write them down. This is your life; you are not fulfilling a parent's dream for your life.

If something makes you smile or flutter just thinking about it, write it in bold capital letters because that's your focus, your purpose. Don't let that go unfulfilled. Not only will it bless you, but the world will be blessed by that dream inside you when you share it! It's your dream for a reason, God gave it to you

RUN YOUR NUMBERS LIKE YOU'RE A BUSINESS

and now you are doing the work to create the momentum to realize that dream.

Friends and those around us can have a huge impact on our actions. We can be driven to "keep up" and we are likely very influenced by the opinions and input of others. Some things can be shared, like family goals, but many dreams are individual and deeply personal. The difference between ours (shared) and yours (personal) is "y"—otherwise known as your why. Your *why* is what drives you, your purpose, and is what this is all about. Keep focused on that why and remember that some goals are shared but your dreams are yours—your reason for being. Your heart and passion. Keep that centered as you dream and think of your goals.

Take just a minute and close your eyes and think about what it might feel like when you have accomplished that big dream. Can you even imagine it without a huge smile across your face? It's impossible not to smile or even giggle with joy! That feeling right there, that is the feeling you are going to conjure up every time you need to remember your reason, your why, for creating and following a plan. The absolute only way to accomplish your dream is to create a plan to get there.

That's a good enough start because at least now your mind is focused on those positive thoughts, and you've given yourself permission to plan for something very big. What you focus on is your reality, whether it's real (yet) or not. Keep your focus on your why, and when fear and excuses or reasons show up, say "hello," and release them. Let them be someone else's roadblocks.

Also, look for the patterns that show up when you start dreaming big. The automatic self-talk, the way your body reacts, the physical state you experience. Emotions drive our lives. When you start to experience disempowering emotions, think of an empowering emotion to shift your focus and energy to.

When I start to feel I am unworthy of the lifestyle I envision for myself, I shift my focus to what I will feel and experience when I am living the life I dream about. I feel confident and accomplished. I feel fulfilled and inspired. I feel proud of myself. That's a much better focus than feeling disappointed in myself, which was my constant emotion in my past. I release that feeling and don't allow myself to live in my past, only learn from it. I don't spend time wallowing in my past; I live fully in my present and get elated about my future, because I have a plan. And soon, you will, too.

We already know one of the elements for accomplishing any goal and big dream is to finance it. Your income from your job will be part of financing your dreams, and we will talk about additional ways to add to or increase your income later and create passive income and earn money on your money so earned income isn't your only way to fund your dreams. But first, we need to ensure that you are not spending more than you are bringing in because that is the number one dream killer.

KNOWING THE NUMBERS

Part of this master plan is to understand your spending and saving. Some people refer to it as a budget. Again, we put meaning and emotions into words, so you may have felt something when you hear that word . . . anger, a sick feeling in the pit of your stomach, or some other negative emotion, maybe? This is how a lot of people feel about the word "budget." That it is painful, restricting, and about as enjoyable as a straitjacket. A budget is simply a tool but if that word feels revolting to you, then we can call it something else! You can refer to it as a spending plan, but I like to call it your financial blueprint.

We can't build this beautiful dream without having a plan which obviously involves money. Where so many people might get tripped up on a financial blueprint is that they list their income and then list out all their expenses and the net number at the bottom ends up being negative. Nothing makes you feel lousier faster than proving that you spend more than you bring home. That explains why we are a financed society and carry an atrocious amount of debt. To not be a slave to money, we have to be the master. To be a master of anything, you must know some things at a high level and be able to execute them with certainty even when it's a tough decision. If you were treating your finances as if it were your business, and you are the CEO, you would look at those numbers and know something has to give.

> **Remember, you do have a couple of choices: earn more or spend less.**

We have two options when it comes to cash flow. We can make more and/or spend less. If you know of another option, please do share it with me. But through personal experience and extensive research, this is my conclusion: spend less and/or earn more.

Which makes the most sense for you? Maybe it's a combination of the two? We all know there are things we could cut out of our expenses. And we all also know that we can make more money. Remember, money is simply an exchange of the value you bring. If you need to learn a new skill, take additional training, complete a class, or change employers or even industries, think about your bigger picture. Bring more value and you will be more valuable.

I recently spoke with a young lady who is working toward buying her first home. She's been with the same company for nine years and is even a supervisor but makes well below what she should be getting paid for her level of experience. If she went to the competitor, she could probably earn 20 percent more than her current income. Just by changing employers! And my niece and I were talking earlier today, and she told me she is moving to a different salon. As a stylist, she can set her prices and the salon will not only provide her clients, but she will also have her own book of clients! She will multiply her income by making this one move (instead of what many people do, which is stay complacent and complain about their limited income).

There are many companies that will reimburse the cost to get certifications and offer a variety of trainings to improve skillsets. It also increases your value to the company. When you bring more value, you have justification to ask for a raise, a promotion, or to negotiate a higher income in order to make it worthwhile to stay.

I share this with you so that you don't feel like you have to cut out all of the things you are currently spending money on if they bring you joy. But if you're just buying things out of habit or boredom, then consider cutting back the spending, if even just for a while.

I have included a simple financial blueprint for you to run your numbers on. And don't forget the things that you pay for quarterly, annually, etc. Sometimes it's easy to forget those if they aren't a monthly bill.

Remember earlier when we were talking about starting with 5 percent savings? Before you start listing any expenses,

RUN YOUR NUMBERS LIKE YOU'RE A BUSINESS

calculate your take-home income out of your monthly income and multiply that by 5 percent. If you take home $4,000 a month, write $200 in savings. From this day forward, you are going to pay into this bucket first because this is your ultimate dream bucket. This is where your goals will be accomplished. This is where your dreams will grow to be fully realized.

Keep in mind your goal is to eventually get up to 20 percent of your income, but we have to do it incrementally. So, start today with 5 percent. I can already hear you: "I don't have 5 percent to set aside." If there were some new taxes applied to your income and you had no say in the matter, you would figure out how to live off what was left over after paying your taxes. But this is truly a non-negotiable if you want to finish financially free.

Remember, you do have a couple of choices: earn more or spend less. It's not just about this action of 5 percent (building up to 20 percent), it's about your *behavior* from this day forward, for the rest of your working/earning life. Personally, I am working on a goal of living off a third of my income, saving a third, and giving a third away to nonprofit organizations who make a positive impact in our community and world. And yes, this is written in my business plan as a goal. I am not there yet, but I get closer every year.

And you will get closer to your goals as well. Eventually, your numbers might be as simple as the 50/30/20 model. This is where 50 percent of your take-home income goes to your needs (shelter, food), 30 percent goes to your wants (whatever brings you joy like a fun car, dining out, and entertainment), and 20 percent goes toward your savings goals for the longer-term goals you have created. It begins with this 5 percent. Decide right now this can and will happen and commit to it. Literally say these words out loud: "Right now, today, I commit to moving 5 percent of my take-home pay into a savings account so I can create the life I truly want." Now smile. I'm proud of you. Your kick-butt life just kicked into high gear.

TARGETS TO AIM FOR

I want to spend a few minutes sharing some good rules of thumb. I see so many people spending obscene amounts of money on a monthly car payment, as an example. That cuts into your savings goals and abilities, and also takes from your fun bucket. Yeah, you heard me. You must have fun! But if all your fun is paying for four wheels, a chassis, and some steel; well, have fun driving around.

Just know that your identity is not attached to your car. It doesn't define who you are or tell the world that you are worthy or special (a car doesn't tell that to the world, *you* show to the world by how you show up in the world as an awesome human being). I drive a seven-year-old car that has no debt against it and that would-be car payment is my travel fund. We go on a one-week adventure every spring and fall, with weekends and short getaways throughout the year to visit friends and family or to just explore and rest. There are so many people who either don't have fun getaways because they "can't afford to," meaning they haven't planned for it, or they increase their credit card balances and pay an additional 20 percent in interest payments to pay for the vacation they didn't save for. Let's look at the percentage your take-home pay *should* go to so you can enjoy life on your terms and have the discretionary money to do so:

RUN YOUR NUMBERS LIKE YOU'RE A BUSINESS

EXPENSE	PERCENT
Rent/Mortgage	25%
Food	15%
Savings	10%
Car Payment	10%
Car Repairs, Gas, Maintenance	5%
Car Insurance and Unexpected Expenses	5%
Cell Phone, Treats, Gifts	5%
Utilities	5%
Tithing/Giving, Kid's Stuff, Pets, Clothes, Dining Out, Toiletries, Entertainment	20%
Planned	**100%**

You are likely not going to see the same percentages from your current financial blueprint. There's a really good chance that where you might currently be on your expenses include 35 percent toward housing, 20 percent toward car payment, 10 percent on other debt payments like student loans, personal loans, and credit card repayments. That only leaves 35 percent of your take-home pay for food, insurance, utilities, and fun (which isn't enough allocated to get you through the month).

Most people attack their funds like this: I will pay my bills, have some fun, and if there is anything left over, I will put it in savings (that's like saying I will go to the gym when I feel like it—but you will never feel like it; it must be scheduled, purposeful, and intentional). There isn't even enough money allocated to buy paper towels—you think you will have money to put into savings? Nope. This is why we have to reverse engineer our spending and evaluate what percentage of our take-home income is going towards those items listed above.

There is another thing I want you to notice about the chart with the percentages. There isn't any amount going toward paying credit cards, student loan, or personal loan debt. This chart is a representation of where you ultimately want to be (growing that savings amount up to 20 percent, which you can do once you no longer have a car payment).

It's probably a pretty safe bet to say you aren't there now. At least now you see what your aim is. Use this as a guide for your biggest expenses. Most people spend way more than 35 percent of their take-home income on their home and car loan. That's why they have to put purchases, even necessary purchases like groceries and gas, on credit cards. That was me for many years.

If you just make the minimum payments on your credit cards, it will take you years and thousands of dollars toward interest to pay those down—but you likely won't pay them down because you will keep using them and adding to the balance. If you continue to just wing it, you will forever be riddled with debt and never be able to save for your dreams. Credit cards are not an extension of your income. We absolutely *must* break this cycle and it starts today. By committing earlier to save 5 percent of your take-home income, you have already started improving your thinking (and beliefs—you are now a saver!), which will show up in your actions, which will then show up in your bank account!

Now, take a ten-minute break from reading and create a rough estimate blueprint of how much you are paying towards the things you spent money on. Don't spend more than ten minutes on this, mostly because numbers aren't very fun, but you can do anything for a short bit of time. I don't want you to look up how much you spent at the grocery store last month. Just ballpark what you pay for each line item. This will help you figure out what to work on first.

PERSONAL MONTHLY BUDGET

MONTHLY INCOME		
	Income (net, take home)	
	Extra/other income	
	Total monthly household	

HOUSING	Cost
Mortgage or rent	
Electricity	
Gas	
Water and sewer	
Lawn/Pool Care or Maintenance Costs	
Cable	
Waste removal	
Maintenance or repairs	
Supplies	
Alarm System	
Pest Control	
Home Improvement Projects	
Other	
SUBTOTALS	

FINISH FINANCIALLY FREE

TRANSPORTATION	Cost
Vehicle payment(s)	
Bus/taxi fare/Uber/Parking Fees/Tolls	
Insurance	
Licensing/Registration	
Fuel	
Maintenance (tires, oil, breaks, repairs)	
Other	
SUBTOTALS	

INSURANCE	Cost
Home	
Health	
Life	
Other (boat, umbrella, dental, flood)	
SUBTOTALS	

FOOD	Cost
Groceries	
Dining out	
Drive thrus, coffees, bottled water, misc	
SUBTOTALS	

RUN YOUR NUMBERS LIKE YOU'RE A BUSINESS

PETS	Cost
Food	
Medical (vet visits & flea/heartworm)	
Grooming	
Toys	
Other	
SUBTOTALS	

PERSONAL CARE	Cost
Medical	
Hair/nails	
Clothing	
Dry cleaning/laundry	
Health club/gym	
Organization dues or fees	
Personal Items	
Other	
SUBTOTALS	

FINISH FINANCIALLY FREE

ENTERTAINMENT	Cost
Netflix/Hulu/Streaming	
Books/Audiobooks/CDs/Downloads	
Movies	
Concerts	
Sporting events	
Live theater	
Happy Hours/Drinks	
Babysitter costs so you can go out	
Subscription Services	
Software/Electronics	
Other	
SUBTOTALS	

LOANS	Cost
Personal	
Student	
Credit card	
Credit card	
Credit card	
Other	
SUBTOTALS	

RUN YOUR NUMBERS LIKE YOU'RE A BUSINESS

REWARDS	Cost
Travel costs/savings towards	
Splurge	
Upgrades/Treats/New Shiny Item(s)	
Other (TV, cell phone, purse, watch)	
SUBTOTALS	

SAVINGS OR INVESTMENTS	Cost
Retirement account	
Retirement account	
Other	
SUBTOTALS	

GIFTS AND DONATIONS	Cost
Tithing	
Charity/Non-Profit	
Charity/Non-Profit	
SUBTOTALS	

FINISH FINANCIALLY FREE

OTHER	Cost
Childcare	
Professionals (therapist, lawyer, coach)	
Gifts (birthdays, anniversaries, baby)	
Child support, back taxes, interest	
Co-pays, deductibles, prescriptions	
Other	
SUBTOTALS	

TOTAL EXPENSES	

BALANCE (Total income minus total expenses)	

Is your housing and car payment larger than a combined 35 percent? If so, this is what you are going to focus on during your action plan implementation. Do you spend way too much dining out? You don't have to completely stop going out, but now you can see that you have to be more selective and shave that down. If you usually go out three times a week, shave it down to one time a week just until you pay off your credit card, personal loans, and student loans. I just want your mind to see where there is imbalance in where your money is going, because there is likely a simple answer to start creating momentum toward hitting your big goals.

Don't wallow in this, though. This is not intended to make you feel lousy. I just want you to see where your money is going as it might explain why things are mediocre, at best. How can we upgrade if we don't know what is anchoring us down? We can't manage what we don't measure, so this is how we can start to make the necessary movements to effectively manage your money.

Your financial blueprint should be something you review each month and revise, much like a business would. Wouldn't you agree there are some expenses at certain times of the year that aren't expenses at different times of the year? For example, December is an expensive month, between holiday gifts, travel to see family, and parties hosted or attended.

Now you see how visiting your financial blueprint each month, before the month begins, is important. You can plan for something big that is coming your way, such as an insurance deductible for a procedure you know you have to get done or an oil change for your car when you prepare for each upcoming month. Once you have completed your very first financial blueprint, it will become quick and eventually painless—but powerful.

There are many benefits to a spending plan. First, it helps identify where you may be overspending. It promotes honest interpersonal communication between couples who are figuring out their combined money situation and also provides self-accountability. Another benefit is that it increases motivation. After the initial shock and awe of the numbers you might see, it should help motivate you to make tweaks so that you can create a tangible goal. Finally, you can track your success as you update it regularly (hopefully monthly!). Celebrate your victories!

When I am introduced to people who are drowning in debt, extended to the max, and have no savings in their bank account, the first thing I ask them is if they have ever planned their spending through a spending plan. When they tell me all their negative feelings towards a budget, as we addressed may have been present for you, too, I introduce the financial blueprint so that they can then see the imbalance in numbers between their outflow of money in comparison to their take-home income.

Once you understand the process of beliefs about our relationship with money, which shapes our habits and thus our actions, the very first new action step is what we have covered here in this chapter. Knowing your numbers, seeing where you can make adjustments, and automating your savings (starting with 5 percent of your take-home income) can have an immediate impact on eliminating debt and balancing where your spending goes. Within a few short months, you should experience a breakthrough in where your money is going.

If you find yourself getting overwhelmed or stuck, remind yourself that you are the CEO. What would the CEO do to

RUN YOUR NUMBERS LIKE YOU'RE A BUSINESS

keep the business afloat and running properly? What can you cut, if even just for a season, to allocate for some other things that might need to take priority in your finances? In this next chapter, I'm going to share my first experience with credit cards and debt and then move on to teach about how debt *actually* works so you can repay it in a powerful way, rather than just throwing a minimum payment and a prayer to your debt balances and hoping it all works out in the end. Understanding interest and how you make payments makes a difference and the cost of borrowing money is going to catapult your plan into action.

CHAPTER 10

CREDIT

Since we aren't taught about money in school, at least not at a level that really helps us as adults, I want to explain in this chapter some basic knowledge you need to know about debt and its costs and how that shows up on a credit report.

Now that we have looked at our financial plan in a previous chapter, let's talk about debt. In a world where we can literally finance *anything*, we need to understand how interest rates work and what borrowing can cost us. This will help us make plans to get out of debt, stay out of credit card debt, and lay the groundwork for learning about our credit profile.

Just because we *can* finance anything doesn't mean we should, even when it seems easier to do so. There is a store credit card for nearly every place you shop, along with buy now, pay later options, ninety days same as cash and 0 percent interest options. But it can become a nasty trap and a bad habit to get into. Credit cards are being used as loans, which was never the intention, and it is wildly expensive to use as a strategy.

I have talked with nearly every money personality type with all sorts of belief systems. We all have our past experiences which create stories because of those experiences. I have met people who honestly believe they get some kind of gold star by financing everything (not a good plan!) and people who feel guilt from even talking about a mortgage because they think debt is the devil and don't want any loans; they don't want to have any outstanding debt. I have seen every scenario from a fifty-something-year-old who has never had a credit card in their life to a young twenty-something that has a bunch of maxed-out credit cards and is close to being unable to keep up with the minimum monthly payments. What beliefs do you have when it comes to debt?

When I begin a conversation with someone and they tell me their credit score is in the 500s, I can often tell you what their credit report looks like without even seeing it. There are the exceptions to the general rule. For instance, some people have battered credit because of a terrible medical situation that created a lot of medical collections. But more times than not, it is because of a mismanagement of money.

Nobody takes on a credit card with the thought of maxing it out and never paying it back. We would like to believe in our ability to manage our obligations. However, it is very easy to get caught in that broke trap that can have a domino effect and create lasting implications for many years.

The majority of the time I see a very hefty car payment (much larger than 10 percent of their income), several credit cards (often maxed out), and I often see an installment loan (which was usually an attempt at debt consolidation).

There are a couple of companies that, when I see their name, I know the person in debt is paying a very high-interest rate for that installment loan, which was intended to help them have a little breathing room or get out from under debt; but it buried them deeper instead. If this sounds like you, I'm excited to be able to help you see a new way to manage your money. And if it doesn't sound like you, don't allow it to be you. It's a painful way to live that feels like you are being suffocated. I have talked to so many people who are losing sleep trying to figure out how to manage all their bills.

MY INTRODUCTION TO CREDIT CARD DEBT

Right after high school graduation, I lived with my parents and went to community college. I remember my friends coming back for Christmas holiday and spring break and hearing all the amazing fun they were having off at college. I was terribly envious and mad at the fact that I was just an average student, which meant no scholarships, and I was the one responsible for paying for my education. I was working full-time and taking night classes and quite frankly, quite bored. In my sophomore year of college, I moved to Tallahassee chasing after that college experience. It sure isn't the same when you're working full-time and going to a community college. In an effort not to take on student loan debt, I was paying for my classes and books. I was barely making ends meet and a big part of the reason why is because I had a hefty car payment.

I had my little store credit card as my first credit card, and I got a bank-issued credit card when I first moved to Tallahassee. I remember needing about $500 to get through the rest of the month and I wasn't able to get my hands on the cash I needed. So, I walked into the bank that had issued that credit card and I asked the teller for a cash advance on it, since the money needed couldn't be charged as a purchase on the card. She was kind enough to pause and explain a few things to me, but I'm the kind of person who has to learn lessons the hard way. I remember her saying something about the interest being higher and telling me it would cost me quite a bit of money in the long run, but I needed this cash. Let me teach you today what she tried to teach me then.

Credit cards have an interest rate that is referred to as an APR, which stands for annual percentage rate. It's the cost you pay if you don't pay that balance off in full before the due date. The APR on purchases is usually variable, which means it can change if the prime index rate changes. It can also increase if you are late making your payment, as punishment for not fulfilling your part of the agreement. And if you have a lower credit score or are just starting off with credit, you are likely paying a higher interest rate than someone who has well-established credit and a high credit score. Store credit cards typically have a much higher APR than bank-issued credit cards. You can use your credit cards, up to the predetermined limit that is given to you; however the closer you get to the limit, the more your credit score will be negatively impacted due to over-utilization. Over-utilization means you are using more of your allotted credit than the bureaus want you to, in their eyes seeing it as a risk with a higher balance in comparison to your limit, so they punish your score.

There is typically a "grace" period which is around twenty-five days between when your last month's bill is due and when your next payment is due. If you pay your balance in full during this grace period, you don't typically owe any interest (unless your credit card charges you a monthly or annual fee, you won't pay anything more than what you borrowed). The balance at the end of the grace period is what the interest is calculated against. And from that, a minimum payment is created. The higher your balance, the greater your minimum payment will be. A good rule of thumb is your minimum payment is often 2 percent of your outstanding balance for balances over $1,000. If you only pay the minimum payment, it will likely take you many years to pay that balance and it will cost you hundreds, if not thousands, of dollars in finance charges and interest fees by the time you pay it all back.

> **Not all credit cards are created equal.**

When you take a cash advance on a credit card, the APR is typically much higher. And here's the really big hit to the gut. If you have an outstanding balance for purchases on your credit card and then you get a cash advance, any payment that you make is going toward your purchase balances, which is at a lower APR. That means the credit card company is earning more interest from you because of that balance on the cash advance. If you pay it off in full, there may not be any interest charges. But the problem is, most people don't pay off credit cards in full. Those that carry a debt are referred to as "revolvers," and there are more revolvers than there are those who pay off their credit card bills each month. Those who do pay off the total balance are referred to as "transactors."

That nice bank teller was trying to teach me a lesson. She was trying to warn me that this $500, which was simply a temporary

FINISH FINANCIALLY FREE

band-aid, was going to cost me SO much more in interest and fees. It took me way too long to get out from underneath that credit card debt. That cash advance portion was accumulating that additional/higher interest charge, and my monthly payments were going towards paying the regular purchase balance (lower APR than the cash advanced APR, although still high).

And the real problem was that card wasn't my only credit card with a fairly substantial balance. Here I was, nineteen years old and already buried under a couple thousand dollars of credit card debt. I took on a bigger car payment than I should have, and once I finished community college and started at the university, I ended up taking out student loans. I was drowning in debt. And if you look at some of the statistics in our country from the first half of 2022, you will see I was not alone:

» Credit Card Debt: $841 trillion
» Student Loan Debt: $1.75 trillion
» Auto Loan Debt: $1.4 trillion
» Mortgage Debt: $10.3 trillion
» Personal Loans: $96 trillion

By the way, "billion" has nine zeroes in it. One billion is $1,000,000,000 and one trillion is $1,000,000,000,000. American households have over fourteen times that amount in outstanding debt and money we have borrowed that is currently owed to creditors and banks. That's . . . crazy! This number doesn't include our national debt—the money our government owes. At the time of this writing, our national (government) debt is over $30,000,000,000,000. By the way, if I had one-hundred-dollar bills stacked, $1,000,000,000,000 would fill a football field and stand about seven feet high. And that is only $1,000,000,000,000. Crazy big numbers we are talking about here. Let's move on and dive into an overview and basic understanding of credit.

I believe that credit is one of the most important factors of all when it comes to financial success. It can cost you tens of thousands of dollars more over your lifetime in higher interest charges if you have a poor credit score. I have watched so many people pay exorbitant car payments because the interest rate is in the teens due to their credit profile. I have had to tell many people they could not qualify at that time for a home loan (even with a co-signer, as you have to meet the minimum credit score requirements if you are going to be on the mortgage loan). I have watched friends swim in a sea of credit card debt because the payments they are able to make only pay the interest charges, and therefore their efforts are not paying down that balance. We don't want to wait until you need credit extended for a car or a home loan before caring about what is reflected on your credit profile.

What is important about credit? In a nutshell, everything. So, what is credit, anyway? It's a game. A game with evident winners and losers. It's a made-up system that we are all forced to be part of, like it or not. It's time to learn the rules of the game and play it to the best of your ability. Not following the rules can cost you thousands of dollars in higher interest charges or keep you from qualifying for financing at all for the larger purchases in your life, such as a house or a car, that you most likely would need to finance.

Credit is often the most underappreciated, but most impactful, element of finance and money. There are some "teachers" out there who say "don't have credit," "don't get credit," "credit is for dumb people..." and on and on. I get why that is the message: to keep people from getting buried under the strangling weight of high credit card interest and balances that take years to pay off.

But when understood and managed properly, which is the focus of the rest of this chapter, credit is key to a well-rounded, financially balanced life. It's important to learn how to discern the difference on your own between debt that can hurt you and debt that can propel you. For instance, you could understand how paying for things on credit cards can cost you so much more because of interest charges and fees and cut into your ability to save due to the monthly payments if you carry a balance—where borrowing money to purchase a home, finance business expansion, or buy investment properties could be the best way to leverage money and accomplish your bigger goals. But we have to learn the basics and understand them better to be able to distinguish the difference.

CREDIT HISTORY AND PROFILE

Your credit profile reflects your *behavior* toward borrowing money. Are you maxing out your credit card and just feeding it with a minimum monthly payment, or are you paying down the balance? Are you paying on time? Are your debts all brand new with no real payment history, or have you had them established for at least a year, proving your ability to make on-time payments? Do you have collections that are open? When you go to apply for a loan for a larger item such as a car or home, most lenders want to see at least twelve months of on-time payments for several tradelines. I have heard, and maybe you have too, of a friend that applied for a car loan and has an excellent credit score, but not enough credit history. To be told you don't qualify for the loan sucks, no matter the reason.

CREDIT

OVERVIEW OF CREDIT

Your credit score is a made-up thing, but it is so very important that you know the rules of the game. I could probably write a full book about credit, but let's see if I can slice it down to this one chapter of information. The following elements are what make up your credit score, so we will overview those elements and then break down a few important factors for the debt you may take on. This graph is courtesy of myFICO.com:

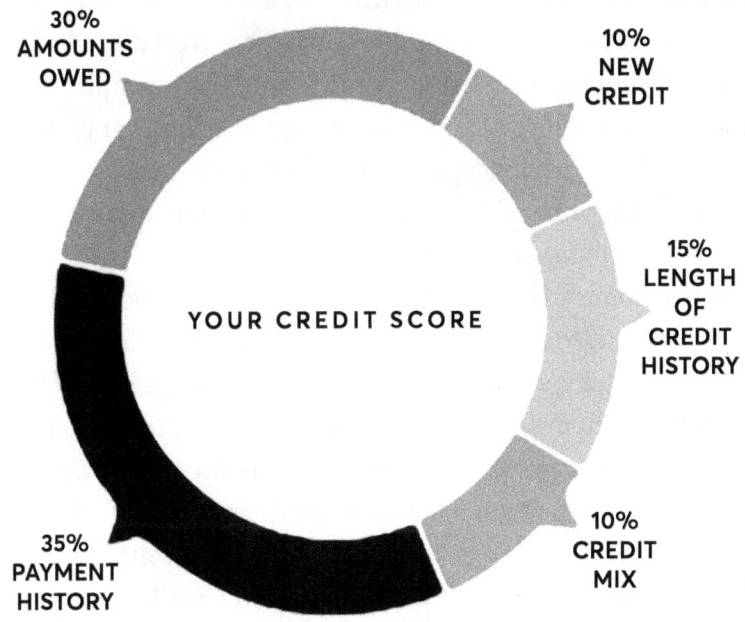

Payment history is so important. It makes up 35 percent of your overall scoring algorithm. Basically, you are showing your creditors your ability to borrow money and pay it back on time. With a positive payment history, you can qualify for more or better credit lines in the future. For example, when you apply for a mortgage, it's important to show on-time payment history on a few lines of credit such as a credit card or a loan.

The amounts owed are referred to as debt-utilization. The length of time that you have had open lines of credit makes up 15 percent of your overall scores. If you had a credit card or loan years ago and it is now closed, it is not part of what makes up your current credit score. Ten percent of your score is made of your credit mix. They love to see loans and credit cards, not just one or the other because those demonstrate different borrowing behaviors. And the last 10 percent is based on new credit and credit inquiries. Credit inquiries affect your score for two years, and you could appear as a credit risk if you are applying for a variety of credit types. For example, if you apply for a credit card and then go shopping for a car loan and then apply for a mortgage, this will hurt your credit score and you could appear to be a credit risk by applying for all types of credit to be extended to you.

I'm introduced to a lot of people who need help getting out of a financial nightmare. I talk with so many people who feel like a slave to debt. Every time they make money, a large slice of their take-home income goes to paying somebody they owe, like a loan or credit card balance, not just to their cost of living like shelter and food. Often their credit cards are maxed to the limit (meaning they have a balance near, or at, the limit allotted to them), they've taken out additional loans just to get by, and they are "robbing Peter to pay Paul" to try and stay afloat.

TYPES OF CREDIT
There are two types of tradelines that will show up on your credit report. As a high-level overview, we have **revolving** lines which are credit cards and typically home equity lines of credit, and then there are **installment** loans which include auto loans, personal loans, student loans, and mortgages. Credit cards and

revolving lines have a limit and a (current) balance. Your limit is the maximum you can borrow. Your balance is the amount you have borrowed; it is your outstanding amount to pay. If that balance is a high percentage of your limit, you have what is referred to as a high debt utilization. Another way to say it is how much of your credit available are you utilizing as debt owed? The lower this percentage, the better your debt utilization calculation. A big portion of your credit score is made up of this number.

This is where most people with a good payment history get hurt on their credit scores. If you use your credit cards to pay all your bills and wait to repay them until your bill is due, you're hurting yourself.

First, by the time your bill is due, the creditor has likely reported to the credit reporting bureaus the large balance you're carrying. The big three credit bureaus usually used are Equifax, Transunion, and Experian. This large balance reflects an over-utilization of your credit lines, thus hurting your score.

Second, you are likely paying interest on that balance since you waited until the bill was due to pay it. Moving forward, I want you to make it a habit to pay as often as you can throughout the month. By doing this, you're paying down the balance during the grace period (the time during which interest is not added). Whatever your balance is on the due date, you will pay interest on that balance at the time of your due date which is now after the grace period. With the average credit card APR somewhere just over 20 percent, paying off the balance throughout the month could save you a ton of money each month in interest charges.

To establish good credit, it is best to have at least one installment loan and one credit card. If you have a student loan, this is an installment loan. However, if it is in deferment or forbearance, it is not helping with payment history, as there is nothing to report. With no payments being made (even though no payments are required), it is in neutral status and not helping nor hurting your payment history.

SIDE NOTE: If you're just getting started with building credit and not really excited about taking on debt to build a credit profile, you can build a credit profile and history without taking on new debt. The easiest way to have a credit card reflecting on your credit profile without opening a new credit card account is to become an authorized user on someone else's credit card. It can be family or a friend, just someone who trusts that you will not be taking advantage of their credit. You are simply borrowing their credit history of that one tradeline.

Not all credit cards are created equal. Some have an annual fee in exchange for points earned on purchases, flight rewards, lower APR, or membership benefits. Some are charge cards and not credit cards. For example, American Express (known as Amex) is known for its charge cards. This means you can make charges of purchases on the card, but the expectation and agreement is that it needs to be paid off in full by the end of the bill cycle. Essentially there is no limit as to what you can charge on this card. Therefore, Amex typically approves this card to those who have an excellent credit score, long-standing, great credit history, and likely a substantial income to not be a risk of being unable to pay it off in full. Amex came out with some additional tradelines such as its Open Credit Card, which allows you to carry a balance forward and not pay the amount owed in full.

Be very cautious when it comes to some credit cards such as furniture store cards. You know, those store credit cards that offer "0 percent financing for XX months." Be *very* careful—some of those have a repayment schedule that if it is not paid 100 percent in full before the end of the 0 percent promotional period, you will be responsible for paying interest on the INITIAL amount you borrowed at the credit card's full interest rate, which is likely well into the 20 percent APR range. If you borrowed $5,000, that could result in over $1,000 owed for interest. Make sure you understand when that promotional 0 percent rate ends and ensure your total balance is paid in full.

Installment loans, on the other hand, do not consider debt utilization. If you just got an automobile loan for $30,000 and in a few months, you now owe $29,000, it's not like you have a 96.7 percent debt utilization ratio (like how it would reflect with your revolving tradelines). What's most important about installment loans is your payment history and paying on time. Obviously paying off your credit cards on time is just as important. Paying on time demonstrates your ability to borrow money and pay it back. It's that simple.

If you don't have an installment loan reporting to your credit report (such as a car payment or student loan), you can do one of a few things. You can pay for some of those things that you purchase online through a "buy now, pay later" installment loan company. I don't love this plan nor recommend it, as I think it sets up bad behaviors you can easily fall into.

Another option is calling your local community banks and asking if they have a "credit builder" account. It is essentially a forced savings account, but it reports on your credit report through all three credit reporting bureaus as an installment loan. At the time of this writing, *Self.inc* is an online company and a great resource to do this as well. The only reason I like the idea of going to a local community bank is to start a relationship with a real-live banker. I know, this may sound weird, but I truly believe it's a good idea to have some kind of banking relationship with a local bank. I have most of my savings with an online bank, but for my transactional accounts, I like the idea of being able to sit down with a banker if I need to. If I need help with a transaction, if my account has been compromised, or if I want to learn something, bankers can teach you a lot about money. I used to be a banker, and when a student would come in to open their first checking account, I would spend as much time as they would give me teaching some basics about checking and savings accounts, bank charges, and all sorts of important things that you need to know (to avoid silly bank fees that can add up to a LOT of money if you don't know what you don't know). Don't let online services replace everything in your life—just saying, human relationships are important when dealing with your money goals.

In addition to the two types of tradelines, there are two types of debt: secured and unsecured. Secured means it is "backed" by your money, such as a secured credit card (you are literally borrowing against your money held by the credit card company), whereas traditional credit cards are unsecured, meaning if you don't pay them back, they could be out that money loaned to you (and get a collection account put against you). When it comes to loans, the loan may be secured by collateral. Examples include a home as collateral for the mortgage or a car as collateral for the auto loan. Unsecured loans are typically higher risk and therefore at higher rates and costs.

HOW TO BUILD PROPER CREDIT

If you are just starting out with no credit cards or loans, it's important to know the only way you can create a credit score is to have something reporting on your credit report. It doesn't necessarily have to be your debt. You can become an authorized user on somebody else's credit card, you can get a credit builder installment loan which actually isn't a loan, it's just moving your money from one account into another but it's being reported to the credit reporting bureaus as an installment loan. You could also start off with a secured credit card which means it's your money, and you are borrowing against it. It reports to the credit reporting bureaus as a credit card and it's a great way to start establishing credit. Just remember to always keep your balances at 30 percent or below your limit. Even on secured credit cards.

Store credit cards don't help you as much as you might think, so try to just have one or two bank-issued credit cards (Discover Card, Capital One, or a credit card through your bank), and one to two installment loans. Make your payments on time. Don't apply for a bunch of credit cards all at once. Slow and steady wins the race. And for everything that is good and right in the world, please do not get over-extended with credit cards. Work to have one main credit card that you use to pay for gas, groceries, and regular monthly bills, and pay it off before the bill is due (to avoid interest charges) so that you don't repeat the cycle.

If you disagree with information being reported on your credit profile, you can go directly to Experian, Transunion, and Equifax's website and look for "dispute" to create a dispute request. There are somewhere around seventy million disputes a year due to inaccuracies and requests for updates to credit profiles. If you see something that is not accurate such as a late payment that you know you paid on time or an address that you have never been affiliated with that is being reported as attached to you, you can dispute it. By having incorrect information removed, it can improve your overall credit profile. If you have a dispute with the information one of your creditors is reporting on you, they have thirty days to respond with supporting evidence to the bureau or otherwise the information will be deleted as inaccurate. It's worth logging into each of the bureau's websites to make the dispute request if you see something incorrect after you review your credit report from annualcreditreport.com.

The three major bureaus are collecting all sorts of data on you and selling it to credit card and lending institutions. Make sure you opt out of credit card offers by visiting optoutprescreen.com or call 888-567-8688. The offers can be excessive and unwanted. Who needs the temptation or junk mail?

CHAPTER 11

DEBT REPAYMENT

Understanding how debt works on a general level can help you focus a little more on logic and less on emotion when it comes to purchases. When I look back at my purchases, I can see in hindsight that many of my purchasing decisions, from cars and houses to shoes and jewelry, were driven emotionally. If I didn't love it, why would I buy it? But if I knew at that time how much something might cost me after factoring in interest charges, I may have thought twice about it. I want to break down some important teachings about installment loans, credit cards, and interest. You may be tempted to just brush over this chapter, but I am going to suggest you really lean in, as knowing this information will help you in so many ways going forward when it comes to how you borrow.

FINISH FINANCIALLY FREE

Let's begin with installment loans, since those are typically the largest amounts we borrow. Examples of installment loans are mortgages, automobile loans, or student loans. This type of tradeline has a starting amount that you borrow, a set interest rate (mortgages can come with an adjustable interest rate but the majority are fixed rates), and a term of repayment such as thirty years for a mortgage, ten years for student loans, or sixty months for a car. The payment is typically fixed, meaning every month when the payment comes due, you know what your monthly payment will be as it was agreed upon from when you started the loan.

Although your payment stays the same each month, how your payment is distributed between repayment of the money you borrowed and the interest you pay to borrow that money changes each and every month. Installment loans are set up such that a big chunk of your initial monthly payments repay that interest, and over time more of your payment goes towards principal paydown. Below is a chart reflecting a $25,000 car loan at 5 percent interest with a six-year term like you might have on a car loan. As you can see, over 25 percent of your payment in this first year goes towards interest charges!

PAYMENT	PRINCIPAL	INTEREST	BALANCE
$402.62	$298.45	$104.17	$24,701.55
$402.62	$299.70	$102.92	$24,401.85
$402.62	$300.95	$101.67	$24,100.90
$402.62	$302.20	$100.42	$23,798.70
$402.62	$303.46	$99.16	$23,495.24
$402.62	$304.72	$97.90	$23,190.52
$402.62	$305.99	$96.63	$22,884.53

DEBT REPAYMENT

PAYMENT	PRINCIPAL	INTEREST	BALANCE
$402.62	$307.27	$95.35	$22,577.26
$402.62	$308.55	$94.07	$22,268.71
$402.62	$309.83	$92.79	$21,958.88
$402.62	$311.12	$91.50	$21,647.76
$4,428.82	**$3,352.24**	**$1,076.58**	**$21,647.76**

NOTE: This chart above depicts the first year of a six-year installment loan to demonstrate the breakdown of what portion of your monthly payment goes towards principal and what portion goes towards paying interest. Note how the amount of interest paid decreases each month and the amount of principal increases each month. The portions change over time, leaning towards being heaviest with interest at the start of the loan.

At the end of this six-year term loan, if you made all payments as scheduled (without paying early or extra), you will pay just shy of $4,000 in interest charges.

What I don't like about financing a car (obviously we have to start somewhere, and my goal is to get you to where you can pay cash for a car) is the opportunity cost that is missed. Of this $402.62 payment, costing 5 percent interest, if you had paid cash for that car instead of financing the payment, contributed the $402.62 towards a 401(k), IRA, or an investment account and could get a 5 percent return or growth on your money, you could literally experience a 10 percent increase (5 percent from the interest you are earning and 5 percent from *not* paying the finance charges to the car loan)! Every time you go to borrow, I want you to first think about the potential opportunity cost that is lost.

And before we stray away from car loans, I do want to share some advice. If you are walking into a dealership to finance the purchase of a car, do NOT tell them where you need your payment to be. Do you research online first to find out what common interest rates are for your credit score (they vary if it's a new car versus a used car) and work backward on how much you should borrow based on your payment goals. If you walk into a dealership and tell them you need your payments to be less than $500 a month, they will find a way to get you there—likely by extending your loan term by a few years, which will cost you thousands of dollars more in interest charges. Your goal is to finance no longer than four years for a used car, five years for a new car, and find a car that you will stay in long term (says the girl that drove four different cars in her high school years). And your payment is to be 10 percent maximum of your take-home pay.

As you are learning, interest is "front" heavy, meaning more is being paid in the first few years than in the latter years. If you finance your cars and change cars every few years, you are essentially paying higher interest charges and not paying down as much towards the debt. It's a colossal waste of money and will set you back further from your bigger goals.

Let's look at a mortgage payment. Now, I want you to remember I am a mortgage loan originator and mortgages are my livelihood. But I want you to know that the cost to borrow money is higher on a home than on a car, regardless of the interest rate—if we were just looking at dollars. And since our monthly payments are dollars and not percentages or interest rates, I want to drive home a few points in the following illustrations.

Even though you may be financing your home loan for fifteen years, twenty years, or over thirty years, that is the amortization, or length of time you have to repay the loan, and the payments are based off this length of time. The longer term you take to finance something you pay interest on, the higher the costs. Generally speaking, interest rates are lower on a shorter-term loan than a longer-term loan (by design). A fifteen-year mortgage loan typically has a lower rate than a thirty-year loan. But since a thirty-year mortgage loan payment is the most affordable, given the extra time your repayment is stretched over, most first-time homebuyers (well, most homebuyers in general) opt for a thirty-year loan. But I want to share the scary truth about how much this can cost over time.

For most people, you do not keep a mortgage for thirty years. Especially if it's your first home, there is a really good chance that you will sell your first home and buy your next after the first three to five years of home ownership. So, although I am going to show you what interest can cost over thirty years, we both know that you will not retain that loan for thirty years. But it's worth knowing and understanding these concepts.

Let's look at a principal and interest payment in the first year of a thirty-year loan. Check out this example of a $350,000 loan amount at 5.25 percent interest over thirty years. Your principal and interest payment would equal $1,932.71. This is the part of your loan re-payment and does not include what would be added to your mortgage payment which is property taxes, homeowners' insurance, and mortgage insurance (which is present if you are getting an FHA loan or putting down less than 20 percent on a conventional loan). Again, make sure you understand that interest on an installment loan is front-heavy, meaning a big chunk of your monthly payment goes to paying interest; and as time moves on later in the loan repayment,

FINISH FINANCIALLY FREE

more of your payment will go towards principal paydown and less towards interest.

PAYMENT	INTEREST	PRINCIPAL
1	$1,531.25	$401.46
2	$1,529.49	$403.22
3	$1,527.73	$404.98
4	$1,525.96	$406.76
5	$1,524.18	$408.53
6	$1,522.39	$410.32
7	$1,520.60	$412.12
8	$1,518.79	$413.92
9	$1,516.98	$415.73
10	$1,515.16	$417.55
11	$1,513.34	$419.38
12	$1,511.50	$421.21
YEAR 1	**$18,257.37**	**$4,935.19**

NOTE: First twelve months of repayment on a mortgage, demonstrating what portion of the payment goes towards interest and what portion goes towards principal.

You will pay over $23,000 a year in principal and interest, but in your first year of the loan, almost 79 percent of your monthly payments go towards paying interest. You only paid down this debt by $4,935 after making over $23,000 in payments! Over time, more of your payment goes towards principal paydown and less towards interest. If you kept this loan for thirty years and never paid early or any extra, this $350,000 loan would accumulate $345,766.66 in interest. Isn't it crazy how a 5.25 percent interest rate actually costs more like 99 percent in finance charges when it's all said and done? Keep in mind if you rent a home, it's like paying 100% interest because none of it goes to building equity for you. At least with owning, your home is an asset, where if you rented, there is nothing owned at the end. Let's learn how to reduce interest payments and pay our debts down faster.

PAY IT MORE EFFICIENTLY

I want to teach you an incredible tool to eliminate some of that interest, pay off the debt faster, and save you tens of thousands of dollars over time by utilizing this strategy. Here is what you need to know when it comes to installment loans. By design, they have a daily interest charge. Because you are borrowing a fixed amount, your starting loan amount, paid over a fixed period of time with (typically) a fixed interest rate, will accrue a daily interest charge. In the world of finance, it is referred to as per diem, which is Latin for "per day." Let's use that same example of the $350,000 mortgage loan above. I take that $350,000, multiply it by the interest rate of 5.25 percent, and multiply that number by 365 (days in the year). And just for the record, I am NOT a fan of math, but I am a fan of knowledge. So, let's push through this equation and get to the results—$50.32 per diem. If you took a thirty-day month and multiplied it by $50.32, you would end up with $1,509.60, which is around the amount we saw in the chart above.

Why is this important to know? That mortgage loan is costing you over fifty dollars a day in finance charges! And that car loan example earlier is a daily cost of interest of $3.42. Doesn't sound like a lot until you realize it's over one hundred dollars a month. Here is how you can reduce the term and how much you ultimately pay in interest for those things you borrow on an installment loan: bi-weekly payments. Warning: more math is coming at you, but wouldn't you agree it is worth revisiting those terrible algebraic memories for just a few moments to save you a ton of cash?

Bi-weekly payments are something you will have to set up with your creditor—the company/lender/bank you make your monthly payments to. Presuming they allow this and will set it up for you, you are essentially paying half of your monthly payment every other week. Do you or have you ever gotten paid every other week? You recall those two months in the year that you magically got three paydays instead of two? Wonderful, right?

There are fifty-two weeks in a year; divide that in half and that equals twenty-six weeks, or twenty-six half payments. Divide that twenty-six by two again, and that equals thirteen FULL payments in twelve months. Just like those two months a year where you magically get that extra paycheck because of how the weeks fall, you get the same effect for your half payments when they are scheduled for every other week. So, you end up making a full extra payment each year, without having to take more money out of your already tight outflow of cash. But here is where the real magic is—it will reduce your thirty-year repayment term to twenty-five years! This will save $67,410 in interest! Could you imagine all the amazing things you could do with that $67,410? Just by changing how you pay your bill. And if we look at that $25,000 car loan, it will shave off six months of payments and save you over $400 in interest costs.

See if you can set up all your installment loans to be on bi-weekly payments: student loans, personal loans, car loans, and mortgage loans. The goal is twofold: accelerated payoff to get out of debt faster and to pay less in interest. This accomplishes both, beautifully!

DEBT REPAYMENT

If the creditor that you pay does not allow bi-weekly payments, you can create a similar outcome by taking your monthly payment and dividing it by twelve. That number gets added to your monthly payment and will go towards principal reduction. So, let's take that principal and interest mortgage payment of $1,932.71. If I divide that by twelve, I would add an additional $161.06 to each monthly payment. You probably didn't know such a small amount could go so far! If you simply don't have the extra cash (yet!) to throw at paying down your debt faster, consider making your payment earlier than the due date. If your mortgage or car payment is due on the first day of the month, pay it a week or two early if you are able to. You would cut out that week or two of daily interest. It all adds up to savings for you!

You can look at the original paperwork from when you got that installment loan, calculate the daily interest yourself, or call your creditor's customer service number to ask them what your daily interest charges are, and then figure out how much interest you can save even just by paying a week or two early. Remember that earlier car loan per diem example above with $3.42 a day in interest? Pay that payment two weeks early, and that is $47.88 in interest saved. That mortgage loan per diem example of $50.32, paid two weeks early is over $700 in interest saved. You will never have to pay because you eliminated fourteen days of time by paying early!

If you have a mortgage, read on for this last example on installment loans. If not, skip ahead to where I talk about how credit cards work.

Flip back a bit to the payment breakdown I just showed you on this mortgage. Do you see how the first three months of payments only have about $1,200 going toward paying down the loan balance? What if you did a principal reduction of that amount with your next payment (meaning, if you add that $1,200 on top of your next regular payment (if you had it available to put extra toward your loan balance)? You would eliminate three months of mortgage payments! In this example, you would eliminate $4,588 in interest charges! Do you see how? By paying the principal portion early, you eliminated three months of payments, thereby eliminating all that interest, because those three months come off the back end of the thirty-year (360 months) term. This is crazy. This is awesome. And you need to know it. This is powerful. Because it's not leaving your pocket to go towards interest. It will ultimately allow you to put that money towards the next bigger goal in your life. Okay, my brain is fried from doing math. But I know it was worth it, because you have learned some awesome, life-changing tips when it comes to money.

NOTE: The example above does not keep you from making the next month's payments. It reduces the overall length of the loan, your repayment time, and eliminates the interest because you paid the principal reduction early. In this case, you would have jumped three spots up in your amortization chart from payment one to payment five. But keep to the monthly payment schedule. You will not skip any months of payments. You just took a shortcut to get further along in your repayment schedule. Lucky you!

CREDIT CARDS

Let's shift gears and talk about credit card interest. The average American household that carries a credit card balance forward tends to be well over $5,000. Let's say your plan to get out of credit card debt is just to not use it moving forward, but all you can afford to pay is the minimum payment of one hundred dollars. Let's use 20 percent APR since that is about the average APR at the time of this writing. It will take you more than nine years to repay at the cost of not only the $5,000 you have to repay, but over $5,800 in interest charges! That $5,000 costs you more than the amount you had borrowed in finance charges. No wonder you feel like you can't get ahead. Sometimes we nickel and dime the things we pay for, but don't even consider that it may cost us more than double if we put it on a credit card and not aggressively pay it down or pay it off in full each month (which most Americans cannot).

Credit cards have a debt utilization factor that installments do not have. Meaning, the more you borrow (charge) against your available credit line (limit), the higher your debt utilization factor. The higher this factor, the more it can lower your score. Back in the early 2000s, before the global financial crisis, 50 percent or below was the favored factor. Now, the threshold is less than 30 percent—meaning, if you have a $3,000 limit then maintain a balance of less than $1,000 (30 percent). For an optimal score, the balance needs to be below 10 percent of the limit.

The two things you can control the most when it comes to credit cards, and the two things that have the greatest impact on your credit profile and score is your payment history (NEVER be late on your payment!) and the amount of credit you utilize. Work to keep it below 30 percent for many reasons—in addition to the utilization factor that can hurt your credit score, credit cards typically have higher interest than any other type of debt you may utilize in your lifetime as far as a percentage, typically in the high teens or well into the twenties as an APR,

FINISH FINANCIALLY FREE

Annual Percentage Rate (the interest rate charged, also known as finance charges: the cost to borrow money).

Here are some of the hard truths to know about credit cards. If you make a late payment, in addition to a hefty late fee, your APR (interest rate) will likely jump. If you are inside of an "introductory teaser rate" or a 0 percent for XX months and you make a late payment, kiss that lower or zero rate goodbye. That party is over.

Cash advances are at a nasty high rate, as I explained before, so do not use this unless your life depends on it. Those checks that often get mailed to you as a "convenience check" can often bite you in the butt. Avoid the temptation. Shred them.

If you close a credit card account that has a balance on it, it can really hurt your credit score because it now has a zero dollar limit but a balance still outstanding. Whereas an installment loan, once paid in full, automatically closes once at a zero-dollar balance but a credit card stays open. Don't close any credit card accounts "just because." Sometimes the creditor will close your account for inactivity if it has not been used in the most recent twenty-four months, especially store-issued credit cards. Don't get pulled into the "save 10 percent on your purchase by opening a store credit card" game. There is a credit inquiry, a new tradeline added to your profile (that can often hurt before it helps in the initial months), and you will pay an exorbitant amount of interest—likely to the tune of nearly 30 percent APR. Please just say "No thank you."

> **Most people give up before they can start to see improvement**

As you have read, credit card debt can sneak up on you; kind of like those (extra) pounds we may find on our bodies that don't really belong there, it doesn't happen overnight. We tend to adjust for it and allow it to build up until one day, you discover you have four credit cards that are all maxed out and there is much more debt than you knew you had—or with the pounds, you can't squeeze into your favorite jeans anymore. It's usually when we wake up one day and can't pretend it's not a problem, that we realize we can't ignore this any longer. It affects our self-esteem, confidence, behaviors, and sometimes even our sleep. Am I talking about being overweight or drowning in debt? Both are very personal, deeply emotional, and can take a toll on our health. Both. Little adjustments add up to big changes over time (good or bad, so let's head in the right direction). You didn't get into debt (or become overweight) overnight, so we need to allow time for our adjustments and actions to really take shape over time. But persistence is key. Most people give up before they could start to see improvement. Once we get some momentum, these smaller increments start to show up in much bigger, robust ways over time. That's where the money's at!

Persistence is Key

Before we move on from talking about loans and credit card repayment, if you have debt, right now is the perfect place to take a pause and write out every loan you have currently and every credit card that has a balance. If you thought the (budget) financial blueprints were an eye opener, wait until you see what is uncovered here.

This is like "looking under the hood." And it can be a little scary, and maybe even a little disappointing. When I am working with a client who isn't going to qualify for a mortgage loan approval, I always spend time coaching them on their debt. Of those who can "prove" their income (they don't get paid under the table, they work for a company where they receive a W2 and paychecks), the reason they are not approved the majority of the time is because of excessive debt payments. Their debt-to-income ratio is too high.

Just earlier today, I wrote a tremendously long email to a potential client, a married couple, for a refinance of their mortgage loan. Between the two of them, they have twenty-three credit cards with balances, four installment loans, and they each have a car payment. They came to me to do a cash-out refinance, to "pay off some credit cards" and put new windows in their home. Oh. My. Goodness. It was heart-wrenching to put these numbers together for them. But I know they have never written out their debt before. What you don't acknowledge, you don't have to (fear or) face it. Just their minimum payments on the credit cards alone were well over $1,700 a month. They have over $600 a month in installment loan payments and just over $900 a month in car payments. That's $3,200 a month just paying minimum payments servicing debt. That is not including their housing payment, insurance, food, or utilities. That's called living way outside your means. And that is stressful. They are literally drowning in debt. Suffocating under monthly payments. They have no clue as to why they feel the way they do, and they have no idea they have taken on the amount of debt they have. It's just fulfilling those wants and not following a spending plan.

Your income and assets are not listed on your credit report, so these credit card companies don't know (and don't prove) your income. They look at your credit profile and see you pay your bills on time and extend more credit. It's disgusting. And scary. It's dangerous, not to mention how much time it must take to make payments throughout the month to keep current on over twenty-five monthly payments due between credit cards and loans. Exhausting! Unfortunately, this is not an anomaly. Too many people have too much credit debt and loans. This debt is often a symptom of mismanaging priorities. The debt is the symptom of not living inside of one's means. If I took your credit card(s) away from you today, could you make it through the month with your bills being paid? For many people, they wouldn't be able to pay all their bills with the cash money they earn, because every single month, they spend more than they take home.

DEBT ELIMINATION—DEBT STACKING

There is a strategy to pay off your debts and we need to focus our attention here for a bit to eliminate your debts as quickly as possible. You have likely heard of the snowball system (made famous by Dave Ramsey paying off the smallest first). I think this is a great plan for someone who needs to celebrate a lot of little wins to gain or continue momentum. This is a great strategy if your debts are a lot of little credit cards or smaller loan amounts. You pay minimum payments on time with every debt, but you have a target debt to eliminate and any extra goes to it. Then that minimum payment and extra you were putting towards the first debt goes to the next debt and carries forward.

If you have larger debts or some with really high interest rates, we need to be a little more strategic than the snowball method. Debt stacking, also called the avalanche method, works by keeping your monthly payment towards your debts the same, so once a debt is eliminated, the amount that was going towards that first debt is now added to the next debt, and so on. If you have a store credit card, it likely has a very high twenty-something APR. If you have a personal or title loan that has an interest rate in the teens, you are going to want that to be one of your first debts to eliminate. SO much of your minimum monthly payment is going towards interest. Get it gone!

Next is an example of debt stacking in order of highest rate (not lowest payment) to lo lowest rate to eliminate debt because mathematically speaking, this will reduce the amount of interest you pay and radically reduce the amount of time it would have taken to pay off that loan or credit cards. Let's say you have three credit cards with balances (the average American has four credit cards). One is a store credit card at 25.99 percent APR (not a stretch—most store credit cards are this rate or higher), the next credit card is at 22.99 percent APR, and the third is at 19.99 APR. And I am going to suggest you are putting extra money on top of the minimum payments because you are determined and ready to get this debt gone so you can start the next steps toward your goals. Let's say you have $500 you can slam onto your credit card balance elimination so you can soon move that money towards your savings. Let's see how this works.

DEBT REPAYMENT

I have included information from calculator.net which is a user-friendly website where you can plug in your own numbers to figure out what works best for your situation. It's important to know your current balance, interest rate, and monthly payment which you can easily find on your credit card app or statement. Here are the balances I am using for the example of the three credit cards with balances:

MONTHLY BUDGET SET ASIDE FOR CREDIT CARDS			$ 500
Info of your credit cards:			
Credit Card	Balance	Minimum Payment	Interest Rate
1. Card 1	$1,800	$50	25.99%
2. Card 2	$1,200	$45	22.99%
3. Card 3	$3,000	$60	19.99%

You can have your credit cards paid off in full in fourteen months! Can you imagine?

Let's look at the power this $500 a month extra you will apply to your credit card balances will get you. The next chart breaks out how to apply the $500 each month.

FINISH FINANCIALLY FREE

RESULTS

You can payoff your credit cards in 14 months (1 year and 2 months) if you payback $500.00 every month. To payoff, you will need to pay a total of $6,805.52, within which interest is $805.58. The best way to payoff your credit cards is to pay back the high interest card first while paying the minimum payments for the other credit cards. The following are the payback schedules. This schedule assumes you do not put new balance to the credit cards.

CREDIT CARD	PAYOFF LENGTH	TOTAL INTEREST	TOTAL PAYMENTS	PAYMENT SCHEDULE
#1: Card 1	5 months	$116.15	$1,916.13	- Pay $395.00 until month #4. - Pay $336.13 at month #5 to payoff.
#2: Card 2	8 months	$145.37	$1,345.35	- Pay $45.00 until month #4 then pay $103.87 until month #5. - Then pay $440.00 until month #7. - Pay $181.48 at month #8 to payoff.
#3: Card 3	14 months (1 year and 2 months)	$544.05	$3544.04	- Pay $60.00 until month #7. - Then pay $318.52 until month #8. - Then pay $500.00 until month #13. - Pay $305.52 at month #14 to payoff.

So, you are going to pay your minimum monthly payments on credit card numbers two and three while the extra goes to eliminating credit card number one. Once it's gone, you will be paying the minimum payment on credit card number three and the extra goes to credit card number two. Then all the $500

DEBT REPAYMENT

will go to credit card number three once the first two are paid in full. You are NOT closing these credit cards; keep them open with a zero-dollar balance. Once you have paid in full for credit card number three, you can move over your $500 to eliminate your loan payment. What huge plans could you actually see come into fruition? Once that loan is paid off, you would have $900 a month going towards your dreams (savings account). You would be $10,800 each year closer to living your dreams! Or you can apply it on top of your mortgage payment to reduce that balance more quickly.

EXPENSE	PAYMENT AMOUNT					
Credit Card	$395					
Credit Card	$45	$440				
Credit Card	$60	$60	$500			
Loan	$400	$400	$400	$900	$900	
Mortgage	$1,500	$1,500	$1,500	$1,500	$1,500	$2,400
Total	$2,400	$2,400	$2,400	$2,400	$2,400	$2,400

or move $900 toward savings or maxing out 401(k) and IRA

I want you to take a few minutes and visit calculator.net and play around with your own numbers. See how quickly you can eliminate your debt and then once you hit your target (is it moving that $500 credit card payment amount to starting your savings goals of $900 once you have paid off that loan?), then you move that money, systematically and automatically by having a scheduled transfer of the money into your savings account(s). I think it's important to see your own numbers and create your own goal. In the action plan (Chapter 13), I will give you some ideas on where you can scrape up some extra cash to put towards the credit card payments so you can get out from underneath them, once and for all.

FINISH FINANCIALLY FREE

Whew! We have tackled SO much already! You now know more than most people about our own beliefs about money and how money is a tool to work for us. You know about the wanting mind, many of the psychological aspects of money on our mind, and your own money personality. You understand that changing some habits changes our behaviors and shows up in our actions. You now know more about credit and debt than most people in the world!

Before we move on to the action plan, I want to share a few last things that may feel or sound a little random to you today, but once you implement the action plan, make the necessary adjustments in your life to move powerfully toward your goals, you may want to revisit this next chapter for some good ole' fashioned advice. It's so easy to just focus on today and not be able to think far ahead or even a few short years from now. It may be difficult at the current moment to think about having an accountant, financial advisor, and people in your life to help mentor you. But someday, maybe not too far off in the future, it will be solid advice for you to consider.

CHAPTER 12

CONSIDER YOUR FUTURE

Let's glance into your future for just a bit, kind of like the story where Scrooge got to go into his past, present, and future. We started this book by going back to your childhood and uncovering your money story. We have been learning some tools to apply to your present when it comes to clearing up some bad habits and learning some foundational finance you likely didn't know before. Now let's jet set to your future. Are you married/in a relationship or flying solo? Do you have kids? Did you finish that degree you started working towards? Are you debt free? Did you start saving that 5 percent (like you committed to) out of every paycheck? Or are you still in the same place as you are today, the day you held this book in your hand?

If we don't get into action, we will be in the same place as today. That doesn't sound riveting or exciting to me. I want to constantly be growing and learning and improving upon who I am and what I can contribute to this world. Because when I give to others, I get so much more in return. Somehow it just works that way. I have heard so many people jokingly say (and yet, they are serious, this is really their plan) that they are going to win the lottery. That is how they stop working *then* they will fulfill their dreams. This sounds . . . highly unlikely and not a plan I would be very proud of. So just in case this plan doesn't work out, perhaps your action plan that will we begin in the next chapter can be your plan B—you know—just in case.

LOTTERY IS MY RETIREMENT

I love it when I start a conversation with someone and when we talk about where they are at with their bigger goals. The conversation usually ends up with them confessing they are not where they want to be, they haven't properly gotten started, there's likely not a real plan, and the goal is to win the lottery. My first question then is, "Are you buying lottery tickets?" And I can't help but laugh out loud when they usually say no. So, the plan is to win something you're not even participating in? Awesome.

I share this with you because the largest percentage of lottery tickets sold are those in the lowest income levels. It seems to them that might be the only way out of poverty. But did you know the majority of lottery winners are broke within a couple of years and bankrupt a few years later? There's an old saying that . . .

How You Handle the Small Things is How You Handle All Things

If you can't manage your debts and income with what you have today, I promise you that a windfall of money will not fix your problems. It might feel like that's the solution, but it will only magnify what is wrong in your broken system. If you find yourself spending more now than what you have, do you think having a lot more will change that? Notorious B.I.G. said it best:

> **"Mo' money, mo' problems."**

If winning the lottery is your end game, your retirement plan, then let's make sure you know how to be prepared to create the solution you desire with it. Because without a plan, I could bet money (pun intended) you would blow through that money in a couple of years. Then you'll likely be worse off than you were before you got it, because every family member and "friend" will be showing up at your door asking for a piece of your pie.

Do you remember in an earlier chapter when I said that how you receive money often dictates how you spend it? If you do come into a large windfall of money such as winning the lottery, an inheritance, or an insurance settlement, it's important to know what to do with it. Here are my two cents:
1. Speak with your financial advisor.
2. Pay off all your debt.
3. Schedule an amazing vacation for you and your family and maybe some of your closest friends.
4. Buy the home or the car of your dreams.
5. Set aside a portion for some of your wants such as new clothes or something you've been dreaming about for a long time.
6. Invest the rest.

FINISH FINANCIALLY **FREE**

Here's the problem, most people blow through it because they don't have a plan and they don't take the advice of professionals that actually work with money. Did you notice how I said to go on an amazing vacation? I didn't say live the rest of your life like it's an amazing vacation. Do you see how I said the home *or* the car? What I have seen most people do is the vacation *and* the house *and* the cars *and* the clothes *and* the toys *and* the parties *and* the upgrades to life. And within a very short amount of time, the money is gone and there is no way to sustain your new life. If you blow through all of it upfront, how in the world are you going to pay the expensive property taxes and insurance on that dream home of yours, not to mention the upkeep a home like that might require?

Investing for the long term allows you to withdraw a portion of that investment, maybe just the interest earned, and live very well off it. Think about this for a moment. If you had $5,000,000 earning 8 percent interest, that's $400,000 in interest a year. I bet you could find a way to live off that $400,000 and still allow that $5,000,000 to earn interest for you, allowing you to have that nest egg and not even have to tap into the principal amount to live off each year. But if you spend it all on things, there's no way for your money to make money for you. Is $400,000 a year an upgrade from your current life? Do you see how thinking it through and making a plan can change the trajectory of your life and maybe the life of future generations? Because once it's spent, it's gone.

Hopefully, you have a trustworthy advisor that can put you into some investments and products that can earn substantial interest and set you up for your lifetime and even allow you to leave an inheritance for your children or your children's children. And especially if you fear money or have a distaste for money, that is all the more reason to find a trustworthy advisor to put your money to work for you in a powerful way so you don't potentially throw it away.

CHOOSE YOUR PATH WISELY

I remember being in a relationship at sixteen years old with a guy named Shawn. He just moved here from out of state and because he wasn't from my small town, I liked everything about him because he was different. He was a few years older, and we had worked together. He listened to music I'd never heard of and had a perspective on life I hadn't considered. I was head over heels in love with this guy. I gave him even more than my heart, and I was ready to change my life around for him. At sixteen, all I wanted to do was be with him. I was sneaking out to see him and lying about where I was staying, telling my parents I was with one of my gal friends.

I was ready to quit high school so that we could live together, and I thought we would start a family. I don't know why I felt so rushed, but I wanted it right then. My parents did all they could to slow down my rushing into this relationship. I was ready to drop out of high school! Because he wasn't in school, I didn't want to be there either. He didn't know any of my friends and the longer we were in the relationship the more isolated I became from my high school friends. After about six months, the relationship had turned abusive: verbally, emotionally, and then physically. Getting out of that relationship was one of the hardest things to do. He would knock at my window at night and stalk me when I would go to work. Sometimes he waited at the end of the street to drive my little sister to wherever she was going just to ask about me.

FINISH FINANCIALLY FREE

I'm so grateful I got out of that relationship, but I share this with you because if I had stayed in it, not only would it have been extremely unhealthy, but I could only imagine where my life would have ended up. I would have been a high school dropout, probably a teenage mom, and broke as a joke because we both worked for minimum wage at a restaurant. He was a high school dropout and even had a juvenile record. So, what kind of career path do you think he had in store for him without a diploma or GED? I'm not saying you cannot be successful otherwise, but I am saying the evidence is there if you compare lifelong income earned for those with a high school diploma or less to those with college or trade school education. I would have likely had the confidence of an abused puppy and there is a high probability I would have gone through a nasty divorce. Not finishing school and being a single parent because I would have likely been divorced just sounds like a more difficult road to travel than what I had in mind when I was a bit younger. I didn't often make the best choices, but I am grateful for the experience. And just because I didn't make good choices then doesn't mean I had to continue down the path of making poor choices.

The choices you make today absolutely affect your tomorrow. Go back to your big *why* and focus on that for a moment. If your surroundings and relationships are not in alignment with your ultimate *why*, you may have to start considering making some big decisions today. I knew from a very young age I was going to work hard to enjoy this beautiful world of ours. Ever since visiting EPCOT as a child I knew I wanted to see all those amazing places around the world, for real. And I knew I was going to impact others in a really big way through my work contributions.

CONSIDER YOUR FUTURE

Have you ever played The Game of Life? You choose if you go to college or straight into a career; you get to choose if you get married and if you want kids. There are lots of choices that you get to make and then there are a lot of things that happen to you that you have no control over but must work through your circumstances. You can end up in a very different place than where you thought you'd be when you started playing. The difference is—your life is not a game, although so many people treat their lives like it's something to watch unfold. You are the creator of your life. There will always be circumstances that are beyond our control but how you handle them is what counts. How well you are prepared for the unexpected is what matters. Choosing who you allow to live this life with is absolutely 100 percent your choice. You choose your career, your partner, your home, your cars, your vacations, and in many cases, whether you will have children or not. Make sure your goals are *your* goals and not somebody else's like your parents' or only your significant other's.

Remember there is a tradeoff for everything. Not everyone is meant to be parents. Not everyone should go to college. There's a very different and distinct path for each of us. And don't lose focus on the fact that you get to create your life. It doesn't just happen around you; you are either on the field (participant) or in the stands (spectator). I see so many people live without plans or goals or dreams. Please don't let this happen to you. You will waste months and then years and then decades only to find out that if you had discovered your own *wants* and your own *purpose* and your big *why*, you could have lived to the fullest each day, getting a little bit closer to accomplishing what you set out for.

I want to encourage you to try to look at those big decisions and what the results of those big decisions might look like in ten or twenty years. Is your significant other capable of accomplishing the same growth trajectory that you are aiming for? Is what you are going to school for going to result in a career that will bring you a lot of fulfillment and still be able to pay the bills?

Also, spend some time in the environment that your education will land you in. I have a lot of friends who are attorneys and hate being a lawyer, but it wasn't until their third year in law school that they even interned at a law firm. They had no idea what the actual experience and feeling would be like until they were already committed to their education and had almost completed it. I've heard this about doctors and accountants, too. Consider getting an entry-level position or an administrative role, or intern in that type of environment before you invest a ton of money and years of your life getting your advanced degree to what you thought you wanted. There's only one way to truly find out if you love it and that is to immerse yourself in that environment, preferably before it's too late with your commitment. I have actually wanted to be an attorney since 7th grade. But once I worked at a law office right out of high school, that goal changed dramatically! I realized I did not want to be in law at all!

I could see that Shawn was not going to be a supportive and contributing part of my story. He was encouraging me to quit school, pulling me away from my friends, and even forbade me to go to a funeral of a very close friend because my deceased friend was a guy. He was threatened by other men, even the dead. How pathetic. Be careful about who you choose to be part of your journey.

Whether it is your career, your partners, your friendships, where you will live, and if you will have kids—these are all decisions you are 100 percent in charge of. These bigger decisions will likely dictate all the smaller things in your life. So don't just look at the immediate outcomes. Look at the longer-term commitment and see if it aligns with your bigger why.

INVEST IN YOURSELF
The absolute very best investment you can ever make in your lifetime is investing in yourself. You have the ability to make millions of dollars over your lifetime. And I trust and believe that you will! The best way to earn the most amount of money is to bring more value than anyone else in your job, your business, and your industry.

You don't have to go through many years of college and higher education to be in a career that earns you top dollar. In fact, many salespeople can earn the equivalent or even more than some professions that require many years of very expensive college. There is such a shortage in trades right now (electrician, plumber, HVAC, construction, painting, etc.) that in many cases require less than two years of schooling or even just an apprenticeship under an expert. I share this because I see so many people go to college to get a bachelor's degree that isn't even required in their field of work. They go to school because they don't know what they want to do with their life. Is it possible that that time spent in a classroom is distracting you from discovering what you actually enjoy and are good at? How else would you know unless you tried?

I'm sure you've heard it said that if you find something you love to do, you'll never work a day in your life. Please take it from me with thirty years of working experience. I have been in jobs that I despised and work that I have loved. It's not just the forty or fifty hours a week that you feel that love or hate. If you are in a job that makes you miserable, it can make the rest of your life miserable as well. I remember getting anxious and sick on Sunday nights thinking about having to return on Monday for another week of what felt like torture. It literally made me depressed even when I was out having fun with my friends. I could feel the heaviness from the work that didn't fulfill my purpose or help grow me. To barely get by financially *and* hate where you spend a third of your time each week is not living at its finest. Focus wholeheartedly on finding something that lights you up. Ask your friends and family and those closest to you what attributes and traits they see as your strengths. Go online and take a "strengthsfinder" test. Consider doing a personality test because that can reveal what types of jobs you might be very good at.

There's Something Amazing Right Around the Corner. Are You Looking For it?

Life really sucks when the alarm clock goes off and you start crying because you have to face another day of misery. This is not what God intended for your life, and this is not what you deserve. Even if the money is good, it's not worth it because eventually it will affect your mental and physical health.

To take it a step further, invest in your thinking and your soft skills as well. I was in my late twenties when I was introduced to *Landmark Education*®. Going through the initial forum and then the following continuing education that builds on what I learned was one of the biggest life changes I ever experienced. I started thinking about things in a very different way and speaking and listening in a very different way. From there I built on some other things as well and made a commitment to myself that every year I would attend at least one seminar or workshop. One year, it might be for my personal growth, such as Tony Robbins' *Unleash the Power Within* (not sure how much longer he will be doing those). If you haven't gone, it's life-changing and an absolute blast! You will leave there a different person than the person who initially walked through the doors. So be prepared! Another year, I might attend a professional growth seminar where I get industry-specific coaching. But I am committed to constantly improving who I am in this world and my contribution to others. I have also found that reading and listening to books expands my mind and challenges my thoughts. I get to consider a different point of view and perspective. I learn from people who know more about these subjects than me, and I get to apply it to my life which not only benefits me but those around me.

Make sure you have a hobby that brings you a lot of joy. It's strange even writing this right now, because this is coming from a girl who hadn't read a full book in her entire life until *after* completing graduate school. But I absolutely love reading! I devour about fifty books a year. Where do you love to spend your free time? What fills that creative side and allows you to use the other side of your brain that perhaps you don't get to bring to the workplace or in your relationships? If you haven't found that one thing yet, keep exploring! The fun part of the journey is discovering what you enjoy.

In addition to purposeful work that lights you up and a hobby that brings you a lot of joy, there's one more element to make this a trifecta with your time and talents. I was recently enjoying lunch with a couple of friends and one was telling us about how he came to work in the nonprofit sector. He had gone to school to be an architect but has now been serving in the nonprofit world for fourteen years, which was not part of his plan, but he was moved by something his pastor said in a sermon. The pastor challenged the church to find something that disturbed them, as in a social problem that they literally hated and made them angry. And then commit the rest of their lives to solving this problem. My friend ended up turning it into his career, but I want to challenge you to make it your passion project.

I have volunteered for nonprofits over the years and felt good about my couple of hours of contribution. It wasn't until I was introduced to a particular organization that had the infrastructure to solve a really big social problem, one that I didn't realize existed but is a huge issue. Since being introduced to this nonprofit (IDignity.org), I have volunteered a number of times, I have supported them financially for years now, I talk about this great organization as often as possible to share their work with other people, and I even serve on the board of directors. I am committed to being the change and helping solve this problem. And it's one of the most rewarding ways I invest my time, talent, and treasure. Every time I show up to volunteer, I get so much more out of it than I've ever given. If you leave feeling that way, then you have found your passion project. Working should be something we enjoy, but it may not fulfill the emotional aspects that we often desire or the contribution we want to make in this world. That is where your passion project will pick up!

Here is your action plan to invest in yourself. Find work you love with an income you can comfortably live off. Find a cause or an organization that you can support and feel good about solving a social issue. Enjoy time in a hobby that makes your heart smile. Finally, commit to learning and growing each year with some kind of teaching: seminars, workshops, online courses, books, mastermind programs, or mentorship in your professional, personal, or spiritual growth.

Here's my last thought on investing in yourself. Do all you can to protect your health. Now that I'm in my forties, I'm actually paying a little more attention! I know you've already started tackling those habits that ruled your life and don't serve you well. But make sure that you are eating nutritiously, feeding your mind and body, and staying active. I have recently started going to a boot camp program. I've never done anything like this before and I didn't know how I would feel about a group workout like how this is set up. There's one trainer and about twenty participants. Long before I could see any physical change, I was experiencing change on the inside. Following through with my commitment helped me feel the integrity of my word. Showing up and giving it my all for forty-five minutes each workout proves I can accomplish tough things. I found myself thinking *I can't* when it came time to do a difficult exercise. But I learned that *I can* change my thinking and crush the goal. Anything new is always hard to start. But the harder you work at it, the easier it becomes—not because it's easier—but because you are stronger. Mentally and physically, I'm becoming stronger. This brings about confidence, resilience, and tenacity that I knew was there and wasn't giving the opportunity for it to show up.

This is so much more than being a certain weight or a certain jean size. I am learning there are a lot of non-scalable wins. Even though big swings in the numbers don't show up on the scale, my behaviors are changing to match what I say I want in my life. I am not afraid to try something that my mind will initially say "I can't" to when there really is a possibility that "I can." But first I have to try and possibly stink at it, trip up, or look foolish. It's taking on the challenge and whipping its butt! That's what grows us to be bigger, stronger, and better with every passing day. Some people just get older. If I'm going to get older, I want to get better and wiser and bring even more value. If you're stuck in a rut and feeling a little depressed, start working out. Especially in a group activity or class. The camaraderie, high fives, and encouragement will start to reshape your mind. The trainer Sarah reminds us daily in class, "You are so much stronger than you know."

> *"You Must Start to Become Unstoppable!"*
> —Burn Boot Camp®

LEARN FROM THOSE AROUND YOU

I think there is something to learn from everyone, from an interaction with a complete stranger to even someone who has hurt you in the past (enemies, bosses, colleagues, and even our

CONSIDER YOUR FUTURE

closest friends). I have had roommates that taught me to be a better roommate and have hurt those relationships through our struggles of trying to figure it out. But now living with my husband, I can be more aware of things that may be important to him as someone whom I share the same space with. I will never forget my first job. It was a cafeteria-style restaurant set in the heart of heaven's waiting room in Florida. The town I was raised in was where you retired if you were broke. I do believe during that time the median age in that county was around eighty! I wish I were joking. Every Sunday, there were what felt like a hundred really old people waiting in line for the doors to open at 11:00 a.m., anxious to get their blue plate special. My first job was at the very end of the cafeteria serving line. I served bread. I asked all day long, "Dinner roll, garlic toast, or cornbread?" I wore slip-resistant shoes, a hairnet, and a red bow tie as part of the company's uniforms. Not exactly starting out in my dream job out the gate. But I learned so much. I learned on my first day on the job that I didn't want to work in a restaurant for too long. It was surprising to me how many people worked there for many years. The dishwasher, his name was Joe, had been working that job for around seven years. I didn't know him well enough to know his job skills, but I knew I didn't want to be the bread girl for long.

    I was there for about a year and learned many different positions. I learned very quickly that if I could fill in where somebody else needed help, I could learn new skills and then I brought more value to my manager and to the company. I learned that if I knew all the other positions, I wouldn't be the first to get cut if business slowed down and they needed to reduce the workforce. I also knew that the managers appreciated my ambition and willingness to learn and contribute while I was on the clock. Some people showed me how *not* to behave because their terrible attitudes got them fired. Some people showed me that if you just worked alone and not in sync with the other people, your coworkers wouldn't like you very much. And I also learned that when I came with a smile on my face and made the experience pleasurable for our customers, they returned the smiles. Wouldn't you want to serve customers who are smiling back at you? I learned how to start with myself.

I'm grateful for those people and the lessons I learned. I have built on it every workday and every year since then. I believe if you show up with that kind of attitude then you are the one getting considered for the promotion, receiving the larger raise, or being vetted for leadership roles. That's how you earn more and do more and gain more. It starts with our attitude and then our willingness, and it shows up in our actions.

SURROUND YOURSELF WITH THE RIGHT PEOPLE

Keep your eyes open for a mentor. It might be a supervisor, or it might be somebody that just has a way of kicking butt in life or has skill sets that you admire. If there's something about them that exudes positivity and you can tell they're really going someplace, pay attention to their actions and their words. This person is likely somebody who gives 100 percent when they show up every day. It's so much more than just collecting their paycheck and clocking in and out. Let them know you consider them a mentor and ask them if they will teach you lessons that they've learned along the way. You will find that people are very willing to help, but sometimes they need that invitation or otherwise it might feel like they're just inserting their opinion.

CONSIDER YOUR FUTURE

As you're growing in your career and in your goals, find an accountability partner. This person cannot be your life partner. Because they love you so much, they may let you off the hook or don't want to hurt your feelings. This person should be someone who's not afraid to tell you the hard things when they show up. If you're being a little lazy, a little one-sided, or falling into a victim mindset, you need this person to help show you the truth. Please don't discount just how important this person could be in your life. They will help you stay focused on your goals and not let you play small when things feel tough. When things feel difficult, I like to retract and just pretend like I can accept being average. I am not average, and neither are you. Don't accept that lie! You will never be satisfied just getting by. You have too much to share with the world and your accountability partner can help you keep your eye and focus on your objectives.

As you work through crushing those bad habits that have kept you stuck and work through the action plan that I will reveal to you next, I want to encourage you to surround yourself with people who will serve your bigger interests well. We were not intended to walk through life solo. It takes a supportive network and trusted advisors to finish well.

Make sure you hire a great CPA, someone who is young enough to be with you for many years as you build your empire. Partnering with a reputable, recommended, and savvy accountant who knows your long-term goals can really help you when it comes to your finances. This accountant can make recommendations on what might be lacking that could put you in a better tax situation. For instance, a friend of mine who is an accountant often recommends buying investment real estate to take advantage of the tax codes that allow you to depreciate your investment. Also, long-term investments are taxed at a lower tax rate than your earned income. So, your accountant may have long-term recommendations for you as you grow your income, assets, and tax bracket.

You also need a financial advisor. There are tens of millions of people who have investment accounts set up at a low-cost, do-it-yourself brokerage. I think this is an amazing place to start as you save toward your long-term goals. Many financial advisors cannot work with you until you have a certain amount of money, usually at least $50,000, and the ability to contribute monthly towards your investments. It might be safe to say that you are not there yet. But once you have your nest egg started, ask those people in your life that are further ahead in building wealth than you for a recommendation to a great financial advisor. There are many advisors that will work as a fiduciary for you. That means for a flat fee, they will guide you and your investments based on your risk tolerance and time goals. Basically, they make a tiny cut of your growth, so it's a win-win! Therefore, they aren't selling you products that make them a bigger commission; they are investing your money in things that will truly grow at a safe pace based on your risk threshold.

I love everything about coaching. I'm not a very athletic person. I didn't play a lot of sports growing up. But the few sports I did play I really loved, and I appreciated my coaches. There are all types of coaches out there, from life coaching to business coaching. I believe coaches can help you have amazing breakthroughs when it comes to your life and business goals. I have a trainer at the gym I go to, and she coaches me to get the most out of every workout. She helps me by showing me small tweaks to get more out of each movement and protect my body.

CONSIDER YOUR FUTURE

I have a business coach that helps keep my goals on track and my thoughts straight in my brain. I have so many ideas that I want to implement that I get very scattered and discombobulated. Coaches get us to our goals more efficiently and also hold us accountable. Don't be afraid to try out a coach for a few months and see what might be possible in your life. Just like the most talented performers and athletes have coaches, consider making that a goal of yours in the future.

YOUR FUTURE IS LIMITLESS

You truly have no limits on what you can create, have, and do with your life. Any limits you might experience are self-limiting beliefs and you have control over those beliefs! I learned to shed those beliefs that kept me stuck through courses presented by Tony Robbins, *Millionaire Mindset* and *Landmark Education*®. I encourage you to spend time and do the work to rewire your self-talk and beliefs. In the meantime, let's look at some examples of what kinds of goals you may have for your life. I want to demonstrate that it is not as far-fetched as you may be thinking to create a plan to finish as a multimillionaire, without winning the lottery or getting an inheritance.

Let's say every year you want to take a vacation that will cost $5,000. And every five years you want to pay cash for a new car. Let's say another goal is to have $1,000,000 in stocks and bonds as part of your investment portfolio and to own $2,000,000 in real estate. Not a bad life! And imagine your goal is to stop working by the age of seventy. How do you make all of this happen? With a plan of course! We will start off by analyzing your needs. We will look at your income and subtract your living expenses to uncover how much you need in savings and investments to accomplish your goals.

All of this is what would be put in a Financial Needs Analysis (see Chapter 13).

Being Persistent and Obedient to Your Goals is How You Finish Financially Free!

This is why it's so important to eliminate bad debt and live inside of your means. It's very easy to become short-sighted and spend all that we earn. But you are forfeiting your tomorrow and your big dreams if you live that way. So, let's go back to the above example. Let's suggest that the new car costs $50,000 every five years but the trade-in value of the current car is about half. Then we need to save $25,000 every five years which is $5,000 a year. Let's add to that our vacation fund of $5,000 and we need to have a total savings of $10,000 a year. That portion of our goal is at a savings of $833 per month. We also want to have $1,000,000 in stocks and bonds. If you are maxing out your 401(k) and your IRA as you enter the workforce, there is a good chance that these accounts will accomplish that goal.

Bankrate.com has a really great section with calculators. You can do all kinds of calculations from what it costs you in interest charges to what you could earn in accumulating interest from your investments including your 401(k) and IRA. I use the example below of thirty years averaging 8 percent return.

CONSIDER YOUR FUTURE

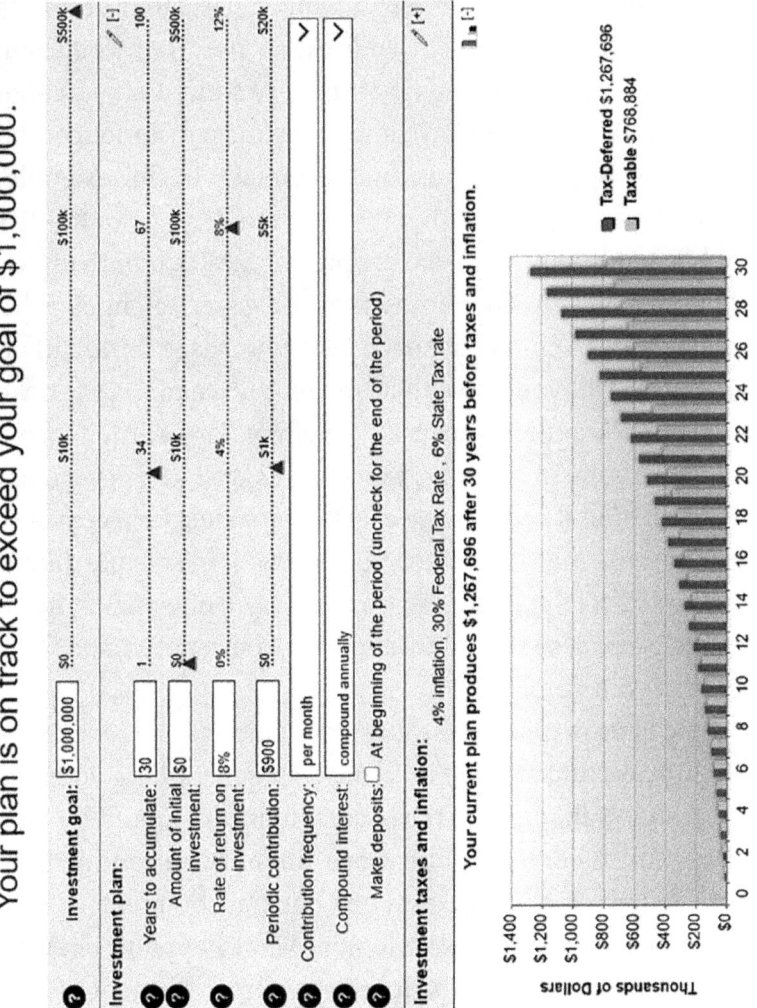

https://www.bankrate.com/investing/investment-goal-calculator/

FINISH FINANCIALLY FREE

Do you see that your $900 a month at 8 percent return will create for you $1,267,696 in your retirement accounts!! If your 401(k) is taxed but your IRA is not, then you should be somewhere in the middle of these two numbers—at about $1,000,000. And if you have it working for you for longer than thirty years, you can contribute even less. In this example it would be $900 per month. If you are maxing out your 401(k) and IRA, it is likely that you are putting $900 a month towards this right now! Keep in mind that the government caps how much you can contribute each year towards your 401(k) and your IRA. Did you know that? When I learned that, it ticked me off! If I want to throw $30,000 of my hard-earned income into a retirement account, why can't I? Well, the government won't let you! It can change every year so just be aware of the maximum. I share this with you because some people think, "I will just start later in life and throw a bunch of money at it." You will be capped, so start early and let the power of compounding work in your favor.

Also keep in mind that these contributions can reduce your tax bracket and taxable income. I suggest talking with your accountant about what these contributions should look like to minimize your tax obligations when it comes time to file your federal income taxes. Look back at the previous chart showing thirty years. Now look at what happens when you give it an extra ten years, it grows your investment account to $2,898,971!!

CONSIDER YOUR FUTURE

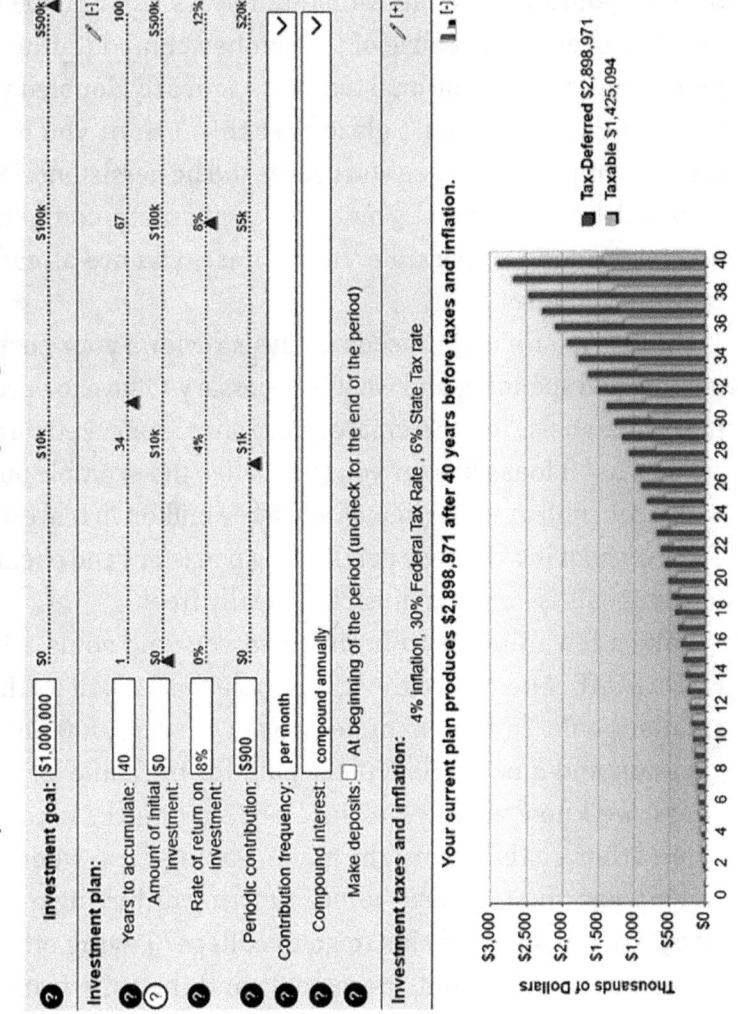

https://www.bankrate.com/investing/investment-goal-calculator/

FINISH FINANCIALLY FREE

It nearly doubles! That is the power of compound interest; $900 a month for the additional ten years equals $108,000 out of pocket, but because of that money compounding at 8 percent over that additional ten years, it nearly doubled your investment. Please don't glaze over this. I want you to see just how important it is to start early and be persistent. Don't stop and don't take money out; let it accumulate, compound, and age as long as possible. In this case, you are already a multimillionaire!

Basically, a financial needs analysis reviews your current income and spending and what is necessary to save to accomplish your goals. You can create a very simple one. Let's brainstorm what it looks like for you (much like the example above with a cool mill in stocks/bonds and a few million in real estate. Talking about it is the easy part)! Being persistent and obedient to your goals is how you finish financially free!

Take a few minutes to brainstorm your big goals—THE END GAME. Make sure those are included as well as those smaller goals. In the example above with a $5,000 annual vacation and a new $50,000 car paid for in cash every five years, we know we have to save $833 a month. What are some other goals you might have? Paying for a wedding? Buying your first or next home? Starting or buying a business? Paying for your kids to go to college? Paying off your college debt? Write out those goals and the time frame in which you want to make them happen. That will help you see the time horizon and how much you need to put aside each month to accomplish that goal. If it's not possible with the current income you can generate right now, then what needs to change? Do you need to reduce your spending? Find ways to bring in more money? You may have to expand

CONSIDER YOUR FUTURE

your thinking and look at things from a different perspective than how you have looked at them before. I had a roommate and worked three jobs to get out of debt and save the down payment money to buy a home. There are always resources and there are always ways—you just have to be open to see it in a way you haven't seen it before.

If you want to max out your IRA, it's around $500 a month, but make sure even before you contribute to an IRA, you are putting as much as you can towards your 401(k). Especially if there is an employer match. That is free money and will grow your savings exponentially! For example, let's say you earn $60,000 a year and you contribute 6 percent to your 401(k) to get a match of 3 percent from your employer. You will contribute $3,600 a year and your employer would throw in $1,800! If you are not maxing out your 401(k) contribution, especially when there is an employer match, you are missing out! If they match your percentage, that's a 100 percent return on your money before you even invest it to grow! In this example above, it's a 50 percent return on your money before it's invested. That's the best return you may ever make and yet so many people don't participate. It blows my mind!

If you aren't doing it already, sign up as quickly as possible to participate in your employer 401(k). Sometimes you have to be with your employer a certain amount of time before you can enroll, and some companies have an open window at a certain time of the year. This will be a big tool to becoming a millionaire. Be ready and get started!

We have come so far! You now have an understanding of your (past) beliefs about money. You have begun to modify that relationship that you've always had with money to now benefit and expand you, and now that you have a basic understanding

FINISH FINANCIALLY FREE

of finance foundations, let's put this into action! Our thoughts turn into beliefs and beliefs turn into actions. Actions will create the results you ultimately want to have.

CHAPTER 13

ACTION PLAN

I am so excited that we have arrived here! You may be rolling your eyes because making plans can feel too committal or like work. Or you may be just as excited because you have made it through all these pages, learned a TON of knowledge to apply to the rest of your life, and are now ready to take action. Let's go through this, step by step, and make sure not to miss one. Could you imagine if a contractor of a high-rise tower skipped a step on the plans? No bueno.

Here is an outline of what the following pages will contain as an overview:
- » Understanding your money story (and your significant other's)
- » Understanding your current numbers (monthly financial blueprint)

» Written goals for one year, five years, and the ultimate BIG goal!
» Open a checking account (if you don't have one) and multiple savings accounts
» Understand your Financial Needs Analysis
» Create a savings plan for your short-and long-term goals
» Create passive income with ideas and suggestions to get you started

Once you have your plan laid out, which could be done this week if you take action immediately, you are well on your way to living with financial balance to enjoy today and not bury yourself in unmanageable debt. You can fund your dreams so they are ready for you when you are ready for them! I am excited, thrilled, and so ready to share this with you. You've worked hard to get here; I know you have. Just promise me something, please. When you get all this in motion and actually start seeing the growth in your savings account and see that your dreams are actually going to become your reality, will you please share the great news and your excitement with me? It will make my heart so happy to celebrate YOU and to celebrate with you.

STEP 1:
UNDERSTANDING YOUR MONEY STORY

If you just read through the book like a novel but didn't stop/pause when I suggested to, please go back and work through the exercise of uncovering your money story. Seriously. Once I got through the superficial BS layers of reasons and excuses I had (remember, your mind is trying to protect you) and could get to the real core story that I had and didn't even know about, I was able to create a new money story. Creating

ACTION PLAN

this new story literally changed my life. I went from earning $30,000-something a year to more than I ever thought I could earn. It's *that* important.

Another reason this is important is because if you are not in a relationship now, there's a good chance you will be. Picture this. One of the top three reasons for conflict and divorce in relationships is money. You know by now my thoughts, that I don't believe it's about money; I believe it's the not knowing of our own and our partners' money story. How can you possibly explain your money beliefs if you've never uncovered what it is that you believe? We all have a relationship with money, and yours started as a little child and it might still be stuck in that phase. Let's rewrite that story, this time with the beliefs of a powerful, intelligent adult. And now you will have the ability to explain to your partner what you believe about money. You can help them uncover their own beliefs and now have healthy dialogue in your relationship and create a healthy plan around your household money and goals.

STEP 2:
UNDERSTANDING YOUR CURRENT NUMBERS

I know this part is probably your least favorite. But it's really important. If you are a numbers person or have the brain of an engineer and love Excel spreadsheets, then I encourage you to go back and review three months' worth of bank statement transactions and credit card statements. Look to see where your money is going. Write out every single line item and then combine some of those things into one category (example: happy hour, your daily coffee trip, and lunches out or take-out for dinner).

FINISH FINANCIALLY FREE

If numbers aren't your thing at all, take no more than ten minutes to ballpark those numbers for each line item. Consider that you spend more money on gifts than you think you do, so write down a larger number than your initial thought for this category. When it comes to the cost of food or dining out, I would encourage you to look at your most recent bank statement and credit card statement just to get a real number; it's likely you will really underestimate how much you spend here.

Remember the purpose of this exercise is just to see where you are currently at. It's not to shame you and it's not to have you run away in tears. We can't manage what we don't measure and so we just need to know what we're starting with. You are the CEO of your life and the CFO (Chief Financial Officer) of your numbers, so look at it from a business mindset (it takes ego and emotion out of it). If there's more going out than coming in, now we know where to start adjusting.

There is a good likelihood that a large chunk of your take-home income is servicing debt—making payments for things you put on a credit card and have not paid off or taken a loan out and are making payments. If you have several credit cards with balances on them, take a pen and a piece of paper and write down each balance and interest rate for each credit card you have (if you haven't done this step already earlier in the book). I recently did this exercise with a client who had no idea she had eight maxed-out credit cards with $24,400 in balances. On top of that she had a car loan, a student loan, and an unsecured personal loan. She makes a six-figure income and can't figure out why she has no extra money at the end of the month. It's because 30 percent of her income is going to pay the minimum monthly payments on this debt. And that's before her mortgage payment! If it's excessive, you need to know this.

ACTION PLAN

This should tick you off and make you want to take action to get out from underneath it. By the way, a budget is required to be completed for those going through a divorce and those going through a bankruptcy. Let's hope this is the only time you have to do the budget, because if we can get your money straight, hopefully you never have to experience a divorce (at least not because of money) or bankruptcy.

Look at the bottom number. I bet the majority of people completing this form will be looking at a negative number. Let's do what it takes to make the adjustments so that you don't have to feel this way any longer. What can you cut out or reduce in order to stop spending more than you take home? Remember this is only temporary. For me, I had to shop for a new cell phone plan which led me to a prepaid plan. It reduced my monthly cost by half. I changed where I went grocery shopping. Although the grocery store I used to shop at was more convenient and easier to get around, I had to go to a no-thrills store where I had to bring my own grocery bags. But it saved me a ton of money each week. I eliminated a few subscriptions and cable. I stopped getting my nails done for a few months and put that money towards debt.

It's amazing what you can find for free when you start looking. For example, instead of paying a monthly cost for audiobooks, there are apps that connect with your library card that will allow you to download eight titles a month—for free! Eight books a month on my subscription service would have likely cost me over seventy-five dollars. It's amazing what you will find if you look for it. See if you and a friend can share the cost of a streaming service and login information. Many of those companies allow several users under one account. I also found that going to my favorite store to pick up toiletries tempted me in filling up my big red cart. I would leave there with clothes and items that I didn't go in for and I didn't actually need. What I needed was about twenty dollars worth of things for my bathroom and I left with two hundred dollars worth of new frills. Instead, I stopped by the Dollar Store or the corner convenience store for my toothpaste and toilet paper; that way, I didn't leave with a bunch of things I don't need. Again, this is just temporary so you can stop servicing debt and start funding your dreams.

Make a meal plan for the week and follow it. If you find yourself stopping at a coffee drive-thru or fast-food restaurant for food and drinks, can you have a little lunch-size cooler with snacks and drinks so you can be fulfilled without having to drop extra money while on the road? We often overpay for convenience, so a little planning at home in advance will go a very long way in reducing your spending. Shop your auto insurance (and home insurance if you own a home) every year to make sure you aren't overpaying for your coverages. From what I see from most of my clients' spending, over 50 percent of their take-home pay goes towards housing, auto, and food. Spend some time on those three (or your top three expensive costs in your life) to see where you can reduce just a little here and a little there. It all adds up to savings that can be applied to paying down your debts.

Start being very aware every time you spend money. Is it a need or a want (have you even stopped to define "need" and "want")? Did you come in for this item? If not, put it back on the shelf and step away very slowly. Notice if something has triggered your shopping or spending desires (a fight, boredom, feeling lousy about yourself or a situation). Decide that you are going to live a kick-butt life, where if you set it up properly now, you can have a binge shopping spree at the store if you want one. But that will come once you get out of debt. First things first. Stick with your decision and your promise to your future self. You are committed to not letting your dreams die and to living your "why" and your greatness. Let's get your money in alignment with your values, commitments, and desires. Your multimillionaire self thanks you and is sending you so much love and gratitude for having the maturity, discipline, and guts to think of your future self.

Decide You Are Going to Get What You Want

STEP 3: WRITTEN GOALS

This is where the fun begins! It's so empowering to allow yourself to start dreaming and to start seeing ways to accomplish those goals and dreams. Let's look at one year, three years, and five years, and if you want to get crazy, let's go ten full years out from right now!

> **There is something amazing that happens when you write out your goals. It's no longer just a wish, it can now be formulated into a plan.**

FINISH FINANCIALLY **FREE**

In *one year* from right now, where would you love to see your life? Have you paid off your credit card balances? Have you gotten that promotion or started with that other company that pays you better? Have you started your side hustle? Where are you living? Are you working out? Who is in your life? What is different? So right here, list out the top things that come to your mind and make you smile.

_____

_____
_____
_____
_____
_____
_____
_____
_____

If you only had twelve short months to accomplish these few things, where would you start? You need to prioritize your time and focus.

If it's related to your *work*, what have you done to show you are truly passionate about your position, that you want to learn more, that you'd like to grow with the company and be a valuable asset? Are you communicating well with your supervisors and managers? Are you letting them know your intentions and showing them your contributions? Are you taking all the training you can and improving your skills to deliver more exceptionally than anyone else around you?

If it's about eliminating bad *debt*, let's create a plan right here, right now! The two things that are the most expensive part of your living costs and expenses are typically your housing

ACTION PLAN

and transportation. If you spend more than 25 percent of your take-home pay on your rent or mortgage (33 percent of your gross income before taxes and deductions), something must change here. You may need to have a roommate. If you spend more than 10 percent of your take-home pay on your car payment, you may need to sell your car and decrease the value and therefore the monthly payment. Remember, it's not just about a higher payment. The higher value car it is, the more likely your auto insurance costs are higher as well. Is it possible to refinance your car? I have seen where someone's credit scores have improved so drastically that they now qualify for much better terms on a car loan. Or if you don't own a car, is it possible to bike or walk more to reduce the cost of rideshare or taxis? If your housing and transportation costs exceed 40 percent, you can see how there's much less to spread out over all the other necessities and wants in your life. Remember, this is not a forever adjustment. It's just for right now.

    I had bought a brand-new car and about a year and a half later, feeling squeezed and running out of savings and options, I sold the car and bought another car about half its value. I didn't want to because I loved how I felt when I drove that newer car, but I knew it was temporary. I was able to pay off that car loan within about twenty-four months and since it was $200 less a month, I was able to put that amount towards reducing my credit card balances. I had to make this change, or I was going to drown. Thankfully that newer car didn't depreciate to the point where I lost money with that sale. Just keep reminding yourself it's only temporary.

    Now take a look at your other debts. If you have credit cards, let's attack them using the debt stacking approach. List out all your debts that show up on your credit report. You can go to annualcreditreport.com to get your free copy directly from the bureaus. You don't have to pay for your credit scores; that's not what is important right now. You already know my sentiment about housing and car costs. I'm assuming you are doing something about that based on what I stated before. If you have an installment loan that has a hefty payment but there's just a few thousand left on the balance, I would focus on that first to free up that large payment to put toward your credit cards. But if it's greater than a few thousand dollars owed, let's start with your credit cards.

Usually store credit cards have the highest interest rate (APR), so let's focus on getting that paid off first. If you have several store credit cards with high-interest rates, let's start with the lowest balance. This is going to be called your target debt, and you are going to work at paying it off with velocity! Sell something, work extra hours, work that side hustle, and stop using that credit card! You are not going to close any credit cards; just stop adding new balances to your credit cards. Stop using them! Once that first credit card is paid off, take the amount you were paying on it and add it to what you were paying on the next one. Although your monthly debt is being eliminated, you are still putting the same dollar amount toward the other debts. You aren't going to reduce how much money you are applying towards the annihilation of these debts.

Continue to do this until at least your credit card debt is gone. Again, if your car payment is greater than 10 percent of your take-home pay, see if you can refinance it or consider making an adjustment to a different car that keeps you paying no more than 10 percent of your take-home pay. I also encourage you not to exceed a 5-year finance term.

ACTION PLAN

This next step will depend on the time frame for your first big goal. If your goal is to eliminate all your debt, continue the debt stacking until it's gone. Get it gone! If your next goal is to buy a home, you need to start saving now. Take the portion of payments that you were putting against your credit cards, assuming those are now eliminated and at a zero balance, and put that in a savings account. You can add it to your 5 percent savings account that you have started or make it a separate savings account called "house fund." If you are buying your first home and you know what price home you want to purchase, multiply that purchase price by 7 percent. This is your aim to have for your minimum down payment and your closing costs. There are exceptions to this rule such as down payment assistance programs. If you are a veteran, you can finance 100 percent and only save for closing costs; but as a good general rule, it will be 7 percent. For example, if you want to buy a $300,000 home you will want to have $21,000 in savings. If your goal is to buy your home in two years, divide the amount you need by twenty-four months. In this example you will need to put aside $875 a month in savings to arrive at your goal in two years. Eliminating your credit card debt should help position your credit profile to a better credit score and lower your debt-to-income ratio to help your mortgage loan approval and secure the best interest rate at the time you apply.

In *three years* from right now, where would you love to see your life? Are you in a job/career that you love? Are you growing in your industry? Where are you living? Who is in your life? Are you maxing out your IRA and 401(k) contributions now that you have worked to eliminate your debt? Have you increased your savings rate to 10 percent with the goal of getting up to 20 percent? What have you accomplished in these

FINISH FINANCIALLY FREE

three years? List out the top things that come to your mind and make you smile.

_____
_____
_____
_____
_____
_____
_____
_____
_____

There is something amazing that happens when you write out your goals. It's no longer just a wish, it can now be formulated into a plan. If you have a certain amount of debt to eliminate, add up the balances and divide it by the time you want it paid off in full. That is how much you have to pay towards it each month, remembering that you are also paying interest and part of your payment will go towards interest payments so it's going to be a little larger than that balance. But if you are working at it at an accelerated pace, you will get it gone before long!

Now, let's do the same thing for *five years* from right now. Where do you see your life? Who is in it? Is your debt eliminated? Are you a homeowner, if that is your goal? What other types of investments do you desire to have? In our next section, I'm going to give you some ideas to consider to start building your net worth and investment portfolio.

_____
_____
_____

ACTION PLAN

_____
_____
_____
_____
_____
_____
_____

STEP 4:
YOUR CHECKING AND SAVINGS ACCOUNTS

Now that you have a vision and your written goals, let's start making moves. I'm going to presume you already have a checking account and savings account set up. It doesn't matter so much to me if it is online or a bank you go to, although I do believe having a checking account set up at a local community bank or credit union is a good idea. You can learn a lot if you sit down and talk with the banker about basic banking information. I think it's super important to understand that if you spend more out of your checking account than you have in there, you can incur fees known as non-sufficient funds fees (NSF). And let's say you had twenty dollars in your checking account balance, and you bought four different things all adding up to greater than what you had in the bank balance, you could potentially incur up to four NSF fees from that one day. So, speak with your banker so you understand how that works. I also recommend not having an overdraft option. Your banker can set it up so that if you don't have the money in your account, your debit transaction will be declined. That will keep you from incurring those multiple NSF fees I described above. Every bank is a little different.

FINISH FINANCIALLY FREE

You also want to know what requirements you need to meet in order to avoid monthly service fees. Most banks will waive the fees if you have direct deposit or maintain a minimum balance (at all times, so be careful here). Just understand what the requirements are, otherwise you are wasting five to fifteen dollars a month in bogus bank fees. You also need to be aware of auto-draft payments. If you have your housing payment set up on auto-draft to be paid the first of every month, your bank may draw that amount out a few days in advance. Make sure the money is in the bank!

For your savings account, I would encourage you to seek out a high-yield savings account. There are many online banks that will offer this. Some of them require a minimum balance in order to qualify for the higher interest rate. You're not going to get rich off this interest paid, but it doesn't hurt to earn a little money on your money while it is accumulating. It's called compound interest. You won't realize the incredible benefits until you have larger balances, but we have to start somewhere! This is where you set up your automatic 5 percent savings that you said you would start right away. So, if you haven't, take action right now and get that set up. You can log into your payroll company's information and add this savings account with 5 percent of your take-home income automatically drafted into this account. This shouldn't take you any longer than ten minutes to set up with your payroll company.

You are likely going to be saving for several things at the same time. For instance, you might be building up your emergency savings, saving for your vacation fund, and maybe starting your house purchase fund. It's up to you, but I prefer to have different savings accounts for each big goal. Work towards having a minimum of $2,000 in your emergency fund. Your ultimate goal is to have six months' worth of cost of living in this account. But for now, let's start with $2,000. I do encourage you to have your emergency savings account fully funded with $2,000 before you start working towards your other savings goals.

If you have gotten to the point with your income that you have your credit cards paid off and your emergency savings account is funded, now you can start a separate savings account. Some banks will even allow you to name your accounts. Name the account "Jamaica getaway" (or whatever amazing place you are going to visit first) or "home sweet home" to help you get focused on your bigger *why* you want this money working towards your goals.

Now that you have your accounts set up, and they are getting automatically funded, you will soon be relishing in watching those balances grow month after month! Now let's look at something financial advisors use as a tool to fund your longer-term lifestyle goals.

STEP 5: FINANCIAL NEEDS ANALYSIS

Many financial advisors start off with a financial needs analysis. This is an overview taking into consideration your current and expected income and your current and expected expenses. With this information and discussing your big life-long goals, this report can help put together what the ultimate savings requirements will be to fund your dreams. It will show your current earnings and spending and what is "available" to put towards your goals. We are also going to list what is needed for your goals that you had just listed out as a monthly amount. There will likely be a shortage between what you currently can save and what you need to save. The first step to getting to your goal is knowing what the goal is.

FINISH FINANCIALLY FREE

A financial needs analysis (FNA) is an overview of your current and future financial position. Financial Advisors often use this as a tool to identify a complete picture of your finances and financial status but also to see where there are gaps. The ultimate financial goal is to be free of bad debt, properly protected (with the right insurances such as disability and life insurance), and financially independent.

An FNA can build a financial plan that is unique to you. The information provided below is just a starting point for you to calculate your savings plan towards your longer-term desires: vacations, education, homes, buying or starting a business, and enjoying later years in life with money to play with!

An FNA can be used to demonstrate your current and expected assets and liabilities, what you need to calculate your savings for your future goals, and also get you to think about needs such as unforeseen costs (emergencies, illness, caretaking), education costs for you or your child(ren), future needs for income in the years you don't want to work (retirement), and passive income goals such as buying a business or real estate. All the while, taking into consideration the cost of living increasing, inflation, how much income is needed and for how many years between your retirement date and how long you expect to live (what a morbid thought, placing a death date on ourselves, right!?). Sounds a little complicated, but it can be easily broken down on the FNA. Ready?

Start with your financial blueprint so you have a clear picture of your current income and expenses. Now, let's list your assets (only list the items that you currently own and could sell for a cash value) and liabilities (debts outstanding/owed):

ACTION PLAN

Assets:	Life Insurance	
	Savings, Cash	
	Investments	
	Real Estate	
	Business value	
	Other	
	Total	
Liabilities:	Mortgage(s)	
	Credit Card balances	
	Loans	
	Taxes owed	
	Total	

Now that you see your income/expenses and assets/liabilities, review your insurances: Do you believe that you have sufficient health and disability insurance? The number one reason for bankruptcy is due to hefty medical expenses. I am a huge fan of life insurance, and it should be (at least) five times your annual income. The younger and healthier you are, the more cost-effective it is. Lock it in for somewhere between 20-30 years. This means your family is taken care of upon your unfortunate passing, and your funeral expenses and their living expenses don't have to be a stress on them.

Now let's shift the focus from the immediate needs you have covered over to unforeseen costs. Do you have an emergency fund or a place in which you can draw funds from if needed in the case of an emergency such as borrowing against a 401(k)? This is where you need to have at least $2000. But make sure this grows over time because illness, job loss, accidents, and a whole slew of other things can happen without notice. Goal is 6 months of living expenses set aside.

FINISH FINANCIALLY FREE

When we think of your future, what are your dreams? Getting a formal education or providing it for your child(ren)? Do you envision extravagant vacations? A paid-off home or a vacation home? Investment properties or stock investments? Do you see yourself buying or starting a business? It all requires savings towards your goals. The problem with "savings" is, as demonstrated in the previous sentence, it's spread between a variety of long-term goals, each with their own window of time. You know how I feel about the word "retirement" but let's state a date that you get to choose your job/hours/income and if you even want to continue working.

When is *that* date and how many remaining years would you foresee to plan for? Example: you want to retire at seventy and you think you will live to be 101. You need to have thirty-one years' worth of funds to pay the bills. Will social security be around? Will you get a pension? If you answered no to those two questions, then how much money (and consider future dollars are going to be "worth" less than today's dollar's buying power) do you need to come in each year to live comfortably? That part is really where a financial advisor can help you with your planning, contributing, and selecting the proper risk-based products (stocks, mutual funds, ETF, etc.) to grow and compound over time. This is where you can start thinking about buying/owning assets that can produce passive income for you or that you can sell for a profit to live from. With these goals in mind, you can start calculating an appropriate savings plan.

Personally, I budget into my monthly savings towards paying cash for my next car, paying outright for our vacation, retirement accounts and I also have a "dream" bucket of savings so that I can pounce on something amazing once it presents itself.

ACTION PLAN

The aim is to be ready for whatever might show up in your life! Let it grow and compound in an account that is liquid (available for you to withdraw from) but earning a decent interest rate.

Take the amount you need for your goal and divide it by your time frame to discover how much you need to save or divide it by how much you can contribute towards it each month and you will get your time frame. Let's look at a couple of examples:

Goal: $20,000 at $500 a month = (20,000/500) = 40 months or 3.33 years

Goal: $20,000 saved within 2 years = (20,000/24 months) = $833.33 a month

Now you know what to save! Repeat this for each of your goals and once you reach a goal, consider moving that savings amount to the next one to expedite that amount. You can then be ready to buy or start a business when the opportunity comes your way, purchase investment property or whatever your goal is for passive income. Do make it a goal to max out your 401(k)—especially if there is any employer match, don't leave free money on the table! And I also recommend putting anything you can towards an IRA to build and compound over time. You will likely need both working and compiling over time to pad that retirement income for you.

Before we wrap this up, and if you aren't ready to talk with a financial advisor yet about your goals, think about what your realistic future income and expenses might be. Assign now for that income what part of it (20% I hope!) you can put towards your savings and long-term goals. Start with any amount you can right now and make a goal with every raise, with every tax refund, with every gift, with every bonus that you put money towards the big goals, the capitol G Goals! Then you can design and enjoy life the way you want it!

FINISH FINANCIALLY FREE

STEP 6: CREATE YOUR SAVINGS PLAN

Now that you have reviewed your financial needs analysis, it's time to create your savings plan. Remember you are going to have short-term, medium-term, and long-term savings plans. It's going to be important to prioritize but also get started on your long-term goals so they have as much time as possible to compound and grow. Remember that chart earlier with the extra ten years of contribution and compounding interest? Could you imagine how different your life would look in your sixties or seventies if you had $2,000,000 to play with versus $1,000,000? I know you might be reading these words, sulking because you're making less than what you're worth and you're swimming in a sea of debt. But I'm telling you, this IS possible for you!

This portion of the plan is twofold. We must look at some places to cut your spending (thus saving if it's not spent) and your actual dollar amount to save toward each goal. If you have a negative dollar amount at the end of that financial blueprint, take a few moments right now and write out some thoughts on how to reduce your spending and/or increase your earnings. I want to encourage you to be unreasonable! What I mean by that is don't let logic and reason get in your way of brainstorming ideas, because those are often reasons and excuses.

We can't get to our savings number until we have money to work with. Are you willing to take in a roommate? Get a second job? Start charging for your talents as a side hustle? Are there subscription services you can cut out? Can you cut your hair at home? Can you stay in instead of going out one extra day a week? Can you trade in your car for a cheaper one to reduce your car payments? Remember this is all temporary. Consider this if you always get a "tax refund" to reduce your deductions to

ACTION PLAN

reduce how much is pulled out and set aside for federal income taxes. In 2022, the average tax refund was $3,039. Divide that by twelve months and it's $253.25 that you could be using towards your goals. Talk with your employer about changing how much is taken out of your taxes. I would much rather use that money to pay off high-interest debt or towards my employer-matched 401(k) than "loaning" it to the IRS interest-free. Many people tend to blow their "tax refund" on things that bring temporary joy and not long-lasting impact. It's simply... spent. Consider using it in this more powerful way.

All of this is to eliminate your bad debt, reduce your expenses, and create margin. Most people have never even heard the word margin. What I mean by this word is "a little extra." If your rent or mortgage payment went up $200 a month, could you cover it in your current spending plan? Or would you find yourself having to pay for more things on credit cards and increase your credit card balance? If you don't have anything leftover or extra—that is, margin—you won't be able to accomplish your goals. And your goals are way too important to never be realized. You may need to sacrifice a little bit today to have an amazing tomorrow.

What ideas do you have to earn more and spend less?

_____
_____
_____
_____
_____
_____
_____

FINISH FINANCIALLY FREE

Now that we have created a little margin, and once your debt is eliminated, you will have even more to work with. Let's figure out the number that you need to save for your goals.

Reflect back to your short-and medium-term goals a little earlier in this action plan. Can you assign a dollar amount to it? Much like I had for a down payment and closing costs on a house or paying cash for a car, assign a dollar amount and then divide that amount by the time frame you'd like to have it accomplished.

> **Goal: The needed $ divided by time frame = monthly savings**

You now have your savings plan! It's literally that easy. You have a number—find a way to make it happen. You will be hearing a gazillion reasons and excuses firing out of your brain right now. It's all BS, and you need to call it for what it is. You can do this. How bad do you want it? I didn't *want* to drive that old used Hyundai, I didn't *want* to work three jobs, and I didn't *want* a roommate. But it was all temporary. And now I am debt free, well on my way to living in my later years as a multi-millionaire, and not restricted or drowning in debt. We take two amazing vacations each year, drive paid-off cars, and max out contributions to our IRA and 401(k)s. If you asked me seven years ago if this was possible, I would have likely said no. But I uncovered and re-wrote my money story and started doing the work. I did what it took to get out from under bad debt and I created a written plan—just like what you are doing right now. And it happened so much faster than I was thinking it could. Just think about it—ten years from right

ACTION PLAN

now you could own over $1,000,000 in real estate, be well on your way to funding more than $1,000,000 in retirement investment accounts, and driving a newer, paid-off car, or whatever *your* goals are!

List how much margin you created by making some adjustments (roommate, overtime, part-time work, and paying off bad debt): $ _____

List how much you need to save monthly to hit your short-term goals: $ _____

Determine now, once you accomplish your short-term goals, if you can then move the monthly savings towards your long-term goals or if you are going to simultaneously start working toward your long-term goals. If you try and start both now, it may be more than what you're comfortable doing. Consider starting to work towards your long-term goals once you've accomplished your short-term goals.

List how much you need to save monthly to hit your long-term goals: $ _____

An example of your long-term goals might be building passive income sources such as buying real estate or businesses. If it's a longer-term goal, give it at least ten years to build towards it. How much do you need to set aside each month towards your savings to accomplish this goal? You may need to consult with a realtor, banker, or a business broker to find out what's required to get in the game. For instance, to buy an investment building, you might have to have a 25 percent down payment of the purchase price. The same might apply to buy a business if you are going to finance part of the purchase. Knowing how much is needed to contribute at time of purchase will help you decide how much to put aside toward these larger goals.

FINISH FINANCIALLY FREE

Keep in mind that funding these goals is for the things that you want to have in your life. This is how you are going to finance your lifestyle without having to put it on loans and credit cards at disgustingly high-interest rates. No more debt! By now you should have incorporated your 5 percent minimum savings with the goal of building up to 20 percent of your take-home income. Listing out how much you need to have each month for your shorter- and longer-term goals will help you determine when to move that money out of that savings account that you have created and pounce on fulfilling and accomplishing those goals! Then you can move on to the next goal.

Your savings accounts should be labeled for what they are for (example: emergency fund, car purchase, home purchase) and they should be in high-yield savings accounts. You could put long-term savings in funds that are invested in the stock market but be cautious here—there are no guarantees. At the time of this writing, the stock market is down over 30 percent year over year, so $100,000 last year has a value of $70,000. There are potential gains, but there are also very real risks. I recommend savings accounts until you have some of your initial goals already accomplished and you can take on greater risk as you have built a foundation that is diversified.

STEP 7: IDEAS TO CREATE PASSIVE INCOME

There are so many different ways to create passive income. A few ideas could be putting your saved money in the stock market for dividends, buying bonds, buying REITS (real estate investment trusts), loaning money out for an interest rate (called a note), or buying real estate.

ACTION PLAN

I have been in the real estate industry for over twenty years in a number of different capacities. I think real estate is an amazing way to build wealth long-term. I will share with you my favorite plan and you can customize it to match your lifestyle. Let's look at that $2,000,000 of real estate you want to own. You could actually accomplish this quite quickly if you wanted to.

When you purchase your first home, you can put down as little as 3 percent to 3.5 percent as a down payment (or zero down if you are a veteran of our military and qualify for a VA loan). However, there are closing costs involved when you purchase a home. Oftentimes, you can negotiate in your offer when you go to buy real estate for the seller to pay your closing costs. If it is a seller's market, meaning sellers are kind of calling the shots because there are more buyers than sellers, it might prove to be more difficult to have them pay your closing costs. But if it's a normal real estate market and you make a strong offer, there's a good likelihood you can get the seller to pay your closing costs.

I am going to suggest that the home price is $350,000. In this case, if you paid your own closing costs and got a conventional mortgage with 3 percent down, you will need to have saved just under $25,000 for your home purchase. At the time of this writing, if it's your primary home for at least two years out of the last five years, and you sell it, you don't have to pay federal income taxes on the capital gains. There are caps (at the time of this writing it is capped at $250,000 if you file single and $500,000 if you are filing jointly as a married couple), but this is referring to IRS code 523, so you can look it up. This means if you sell your home and your home value has increased and you get $100,000 out of your home, you do not have to pay any capital gains when you sell! So, you can live in it for two years and sell it and any gains you earn are tax-free! But the best way to build a real estate portfolio is the following.

When you are shopping for your first home, don't look at it as your forever home, because it's not going to be! Look through the eyes of a tenant. Is it a good home in a good neighborhood near the things a household would want to be near such as shopping, schools, and parks? When you buy your first home as your primary residence, remember you only have to put down a minimum of 3 percent. You are considered a first-time home buyer if you've never owned a home or 'real estate in the last three years. You can have an FHA loan, even if it's not your first home with as little as 3.5 percent down. Buy this home and live in it for at least one year. Mortgage underwriters will not give you a hard time if it's been your primary residence for one year before you go to buy your next home as your next primary residence. If it's less than one year, it opens a can of worms with some questions you'll have to answer (side note: if you get a job transfer or your family expands and you have outgrown your home sooner than one year, that is a good enough reason to buy a different home in less than one year).

Set a goal of when you want to buy your next home. This will help you in formulating how much you need to save for your next home. Your next primary home will require 5 percent down on a conventional mortgage plus closing costs. So, in this case, let's save up to 9 percent of your next primary home purchase price to cover your down payment and closing costs. If you are working towards building a real estate empire, figure out what property type works best for you. A

ACTION PLAN

good place to start is a single-family home with three bedrooms and two bathrooms with a price that does not exceed the average-priced home in your area. Another investment consideration is a home with an accessory dwelling unit. This means a secondary structure on the property that can be rented out while you live in the home. This is an excellent way to offset your mortgage payment and expedite your savings plans if you put all that rent aside in savings. Some people like multifamily homes. You can get a regular conventional mortgage loan on a single-family home, a duplex, a triplex, or a fourplex. Once it is larger than four units, it's not a standard Fannie Mae or Freddie Mac bank loan. I encourage you to look at four units or less.

If you buy a multifamily home, your down payment on a conventional mortgage increases to a 15 percent down payment. If you are planning on buying a multifamily home, consider an FHA loan, as it still requires only a 3.5 percent down payment. In most cases, you can only have one FHA loan at a time (one exception to the rule is requiring 30 percent equity, more than a hundred miles from your first home, and having an appraisal done—it's kind of a pain!). If you buy a multifamily home, remember you have to live in one of the units as your primary residence for this minimal down payment.

Let's get back to your goal of when you want to buy your home. Let's say you want to buy your next home in two years and you're going to stay with a sales price of $350,000. You're going to have a 5 percent down payment and closing costs, so I would anticipate having $31,000 in savings towards the purchase of your next home. If your goal is to purchase in two years, you need to save about $1,300 a month toward your next home purchase. I know this may sound like a lot, but if you wound up buying your next home as a rental property/investment property, you would have to put 20 percent down payment plus closing costs. Twenty percent of $350,000 is a $70,000 down payment and when you add closing costs, your out-of-pocket far exceeds $80,000. WOAH! That $31,000 doesn't look so bad now!

When you go to buy your next home, you will need to have a lease agreement and a security deposit for your first home to be rented out. Seventy-five percent of your rental income can be used to offset that mortgage payment of your first home when you convert it to the rental property. So, let's say your mortgage payment is $2,500 and you can rent it out for $3,000 a month. We can apply $2,250 against your $2,500 mortgage payment, making you only liable for $250 added to your debt-to-income ratio! Amazing! If you utilize this strategy every two years, in twelve years from the date of your first purchase, you will own $2,100,000 in real estate, even before it appreciates! I am assuming a $350,000 purchase price for every home. Have fun with this right now—choose the purchase price for your home or start with a small purchase price for your first home and maybe increase the value for each home by $50,000 or $100,000. See how much real estate you can own over the next couple of decades!

Personally, I want to buy a $400,000 value home every two years and in thirty years from right now, we will own $6,000,000 in real estate. I personally have no intention of managing the properties. I will hire a property manager to take care of everything. Mortgage guidelines actually require six months' worth of reserves (cash money in savings equal to six months' worth of housing payments) for each property you own if you are financing an investment home. A good rule of thumb is to not buy your next property until you have saved an additional six months of reserves for each property you own. Why not hedge your risk of missing payments if your tenant does not pay their rent?

Our goal is not necessarily to make money off the rent each month, although that may be a goal of yours. You want to have the real estate paid off by the time you retire from working. Then you can cash flow on every property at a maximum amount. With that mortgage paid off, you would only be responsible for taxes and insurance.

Let's think about this for a minute. Let's say you can get $2,500 in rent and once the mortgage is paid off a few decades from right now, and you only have to pay for taxes and insurance, you could likely cash flow $2,000 per property. That's $10,000 a month if you own those five rental/investment properties (because one home is now your primary home). This is an amazing and predictable way to create passive income.

> *When you stop working you stop earning, unless you have investments.*

As we know, the stock market can be very volatile and often unpredictable. But real estate seems to be very steady long-term. If you see that prices are heightened and it feels like a peak, postpone buying an investment property at that moment in time. What goes up must come down. When there is a change in the economy, likely due to a recession or some kind of economic event, when real estate decreases in value, purchase as much as you're able to. If you have not read Robert Kiyosaki's *Rich Dad, Poor Dad*, I highly recommend it. It was life-changing for me and he goes into greater detail on building wealth through real estate. He also teaches the four ways to earn income. It's so much more than the income you create from your job. But the majority of people get stuck there. When you read his book, you will learn that you can earn income from your job, by being self-employed, by owning a business, and by owning investments. Most people remain a slave to their job and if they didn't save any money or contribute towards their retirement accounts, they have no money coming in when they stop working. It breaks my heart when I talk to people who collect $1,200 to $1,500 a month in Social Security and have no other income. It was not intended for us to live off and it's not enough to live off.

Passive income basically means having your money work for more money. This might be through putting money in the stock market and getting dividends, buying bonds that pay interest, buying REITS (real estate investment trusts), loaning money out for an interest rate (called a note), or owning real estate, to name a few examples. What you will find as examples of passive income is usually an investment into something or a side hustle. But this will help you ween off relying on the income you generate. The takeaway here is that you utilize your money (savings) to grow and make money from your money, so you can stop working for your money, and your money works for you!

Let's shift and talk about the stock market. To me, I feel like it is a bit more speculative than real estate, although

ACTION PLAN

you never want to have all your eggs in one basket. It's so important to diversify. If you are going to invest money in the stock market, my suggestion is not to hold individual stocks. Any company could have an internal disrupter, like a corrupt leader embezzling company funds or an external industry change that diminishes the stock value. My recommendation is to follow the recommendation of your financial advisor. Also consider asking about being in a fund or an index that has a mix of large, small, domestic, and international companies that is well diversified. Your goal is for your money to grow, slow and steady, hedging volatility as much as possible. I hear people trying to "beat the market" all the time—they try to day trade or chase stock selections, attempting to earn higher returns than the average. I say that with stocks, average is great. You can count on a steady 8 to 10 percent long-term return on your investment in well-diversified funds. That's a great return; don't risk your money chasing after a rainbow. Buy when the stock market is low; sell when it is high. It is literally impossible to time the market. Warren Buffett, one of the richest men in the world says to do the opposite of what everyone else is doing. When others are selling (fear-driven and scarcity-minded), you should be buying. Again, diversification is key. Don't go all in on the stock market; don't go all in on real estate or a business. Spread the love.

Make sure before you go investing any money in these various types of investments that your debt is paid off, you are saving at least 10 percent of your income, and you have at least six months of living expenses in your emergency fund. That's the only way to weather a storm. And there will always be storms. There are ways to protect your investments and

FINISH FINANCIALLY FREE

assets. Having savings and no debt is mandatory before you start sticking your money into investments that don't come with a "money-back guarantee." It is taking a gamble and can be speculative, so having savings is required.

Are you taking action? Decide to start today. No more reasons and excuses. No more procrastination. Watch your life drastically change! When we can master our money, everything else seems to align as well. The stress is removed, work is enjoyable, and we don't lose sleep worrying about how to pay the bills. Our health, mind, and bank accounts seem to be healthier.

Something that will be important is having accountability. Join our collaborative community to share ideas, share successes, and ask for support when needed. It's not always easy, as there will be plenty of mountains to move and roadblocks thrown in the mix. Stay persistent. Don't quit. Stay focused on your why. Feel your purpose and keep your energy fixated on what you want (don't focus on what you *don't* want).

> *"To Create One's Own World Takes Courage."*
> *—Georgia O'Keefe*

BONUS CHAPTER

RECESSION-PROOF YOUR LIFE

Nothing is scarier than outside factors destroying what you have worked so hard for, and you have no say in the matter. But you can be as prepared as possible. Before anything else, have your *emergency savings*. Your very first step is to have $2,000 in an emergency fund. That can cover most surprises. Your ultimate goal is to have six months of living expenses in your emergency fund. That can cover life's most unexpected experiences: unemployment, business failure, illness, death of a loved one, and recovery time from an injury or surgery.

Know your spending by completing that financial blueprint (you know, your budget) to see where you can cut back. If you spend every penny you earn, you are setting yourself up for disaster. What if your employer chooses to reduce everyone's forty-hour work week down to thirty-two hours in an effort to not eliminate any positions? Can you live off the reduced income? Likely not for long.

Eliminate high-interest credit cards—pay off those balances ASAP.

Don't be in the mindset that your job and income will always be there. Learn to live off your base pay (if you earn overtime, bonus, or commission income) because that "extra" income can be gone in an instant. I have personally experienced that, and it is devastating.

Avoid speculative "investing" in a volatile market.

Cut back temporarily on the luxuries you may have been treating yourself to when times are good. Recessions are not permanent. You can go back to enjoying your indulgences on the other side of it.

Stay away from the mall, retail stores, or whatever may tempt you to spend money on wants and not needs.

Get a side hustle or pick up a side job to insulate from possible main income reduction or to stockpile up some savings.

Stay healthy. It can be easy to slip into a mindset of scarcity or fear. Workout, keep your body moving and fueled with nutritious foods, and don't get caught up in a bad habit of drinking or medicating anxious feelings away. Your physical health absolutely affects your mental health (and vice versa). Remember your self-worth has nothing to do with your net worth.

If you do lose your job, communicate this with your creditors and many times they will offer a temporary time of not having to make payments towards your bills. It is often referred to as a forbearance and can provide a few months of skipping payments without harming your credit profile. You must communicate with your creditors; don't just be late on your payments as that will destroy your credit. If you are late on one bill and it's reported on your credit, your other creditors have a right (and they use it!) to tap into your credit profile and see what is going on. If they see you are late, that may cause them to panic a little and I have seen credit cards reduce the limit available to you. This will then punish you more because you can no longer access the limit you previously had available and your debt utilization also decreases, which can further hurt your credit scores.

Make a needs list and walk in with a designated amount of money for your purchase. Make a commitment not to exceed the amount that is alloted for. If you go over on cost, put something back. It's like tough love in action.

Consider shopping at a different store than you usually do. Grocery shop at a store that carries generic brands or buy your toiletries at a discount retailer such as Big Lots or Ollies. Just don't put things in your car that are a want—you are only there for your needs.

Are there things you can sell to get by during this time? If you lose your job and therefore your income, you may not value those season football tickets the same as you did when you had income flowing in.

Meal prep. I can't tell you how much money I have thrown away because I got dinner delivered in because I didn't have groceries at home or have thrown food away because I over-purchased on produce and didn't get to it on time. Planning meals for the week (and being aware of the meals you won't be around for as to not over-buy) can save you a lot of money on food.

Shop insurances. Car and homeowners' insurance combined can cost hundreds a month. Shop every year before their renewal date (typically one to two months prior to your renewal date) and see if you can find some savings there.

Pay attention to how you pay. You often spend more on a credit card than if you are paying cash. Be aware of what you are spending money on.

Create disrupters that make you pause and think before you make a purchase or agree to something. A good rule of thumb is if you are going to spend more than one hundred dollars, commit to waiting for twenty-four hours before you go through with the purchase.

Be honest with those in your life. If things are tight, and you get invited to something that will cost you money you don't have to put toward that event, be honest. You don't have to impress anyone.

Don't risk what you have chasing after some hoax, tip, or promise that a friend says will be the answer. Just stay focused on your goals, stay afloat, do not spend more than absolutely necessary, and do not get buried (again?) in debt.

Feelings drive decisions. Keep your feelings in check by checking in to see what is driving that decision. It's often a desire to feel happiness. Usually, a purchase won't provide long-term happiness. It's fleeting and it costs you.

Express gratitude for the things you do have and will have. It's easy to get trapped in the wanting mind and yearning for what you don't have. But don't forget to appreciate and show gratefulness for what you do have. There are millions of people around the world that would kill to be in your name-brand shoes and living your life. Let's not take things for granted. Things are tough—so what? We still have it better than most of the rest of the world. Remember that our problems are first-world problems. Go on a mission trip to a third-world country and tell me if you come back with the same views. Your needs list will change, I can promise you that!

Teach the Brain. Train the Mind.

CLOSING

Thank you so much for being with me on this journey. I trust that you learned a lot about yourself and how your past can really control your future unless we gain understanding, create a new story and then get into action. I truly believe the level of success we can achieve in our years here on earth is a product of the right mindset. You have done a tremendous amount of work on personal development through these pages. By growing our knowledge of ourself, and then creating an action plan to help us with each step towards our short- and long-term goals, we can experience the kind of life that earlier may have felt unattainable. You can create it. You will create it. When you are financially free, you can bless others, live with less stress and enjoy the beauty of the world around us. I'm proud of you for putting in the work to create the life you envision for yourself and your family.

FINISH FINANCIALLY FREE

I am already working on my next projects. Let's connect so you know when the next book comes out. I will be building on this foundation and offering more pinpointed topics for finishing financially free such as for couples, recent grads, divorces, and bankruptcy. Learn more at www.creditkristi.com.

www.ingramcontent.com/pod-product-compliance
Lightning Source LLC
Chambersburg PA
CBHW050521170426
43201CB00013B/2035